ADVANCE PRAISE

"School leaders are in the crosshairs of a divided nation, holding our communities together during the most challenging period of our lifetimes. Dr. Largent gives practical tips, guidance, and, yes, even hope for those of us who are committed to serving our nation's children and, ultimately, our future. No message could be more timely, practical, or important than this."

—KEVIN BROWN, Executive Director, Texas Association of School Administrators, former superintendent

"I have known Dr. Largent since I was a high school student and he was my high school assistant principal. I have always been inspired by his leadership. In his book, Leading in Chaos, he provides guidance and wise counsel to those interested in becoming school leaders. I highly recommend that all aspiring leaders read this book for the encouragement they will need for the challenges they will face."

—DR. LATONYA GOFFNEY, Texas Superintendent of the Year 2017, superintendent, Aldine ISD, President-Elect, Texas Association of School Administrators

"My friend and fellow superintendent of schools, Dr. Jim Largent has written an invaluable guide for current and aspiring school leaders who want to better find their way—and understand their obligations—in today's divided political climate. Dr. Largent has a down-to-earth style and the kind of pragmatic, accessible wisdom that can only come from years of experience doing the very thing he writes about.

Dr. Largent does us all a service by laying out a clear, understandable, and proven roadmap to help educational leaders navigate their teams through the chaos around them.The world's crazy, but school leaders don't have to be. Leading in Chaos is an invaluable tool for keeping your cool as you lead your school. Highly recommended."

—DR. JOHN KUHN, author, superintendent, Mineral Wells ISD

"This book comes at a time when many school leaders are questioning the importance of the job they do, considering the current culture wars going on in our country. In this book, Dr. Largent provides a blueprint for how to lead, even in these stressful times. This is a must-read."

—DR. MICHAEL HOLLAND, Executive Director-Region VI Education Service Center, former Texas school superintendent

"Working for Dr. Largent prepared me for the issues that lie ahead in the role of superintendent. I am excited that he now shares with everyone his commonsense approach to tackling the challenges that we face as school leaders. This is a must-read for all leaders in public education."

—RON HOLMGREEN, superintendent, Brock ISD

"I had the privilege of serving under Dr. Largent for six years. Every word in this book is reflective of his leadership, which has proven successful time and time again. Being able to learn and grow from him firsthand, I can tell you that this book is absolute gold. It is a must-read for all aspiring and current administrators seeking to advance in school leadership."

—ANNA ROE, Director of Teaching and Learning, Crowley ISD

LEADING
IN
CHAOS

LEADING
IN
CHAOS

A Commonsense Blueprint for
New and Aspiring School Leaders

Dr. Jim Largent

HOUNDSTOOTH
PRESS

LEADING IN CHAOS
A Commonsense Blueprint for New and Aspiring School Leaders

ISBN   978-1-5445-3321-6   *Hardcover*

        978-1-5445-3322-3   *Paperback*

        978-1-5445-3323-0   *Ebook*

CONTENTS

To Justin and Jaci.
My wish for you is that you find a job
and career path you love, so you will never have to
work a day in your life. Life is too short.
Find your passion and enjoy the ride!

ACKNOWLEDGMENTS

IN ORDER TO BE SUCCESSFUL IN ANY LEADERSHIP ROLE, it is important to have mentors and people to lean on. In this book, I wrote about specific people and how they helped me. In addition, I want to thank Brian Zemlicka, Phil Worsham, Gene Isabell, Lowell McQuistion, Jimmy Chapman, and the patriarch of Nacogdoches County, Ford King, for their friendship, help, and guidance in my first years as a superintendent.

I also want to acknowledge all the wonderful educators and support staff I have had the pleasure of working with my entire professional life. I have worked with many amazing leaders, extraordinary people, and those whose calling is to serve the children in public schools. Thank you for the work you do every day to help our kids achieve their American dream!

Thanks to everyone on the Scribe team. From the editors, cover designers, proofreaders, quality assurance team, and layout specialists. Special thanks to Eliece, my publishing manager, who kept me on track, and Miles, who helped me begin my journey with Scribe.

To Mom and Dad and my "3 Js," my wife, Jeri, and our two wonderful kids, Justin and Jaci. Thanks for always supporting me in my professional endeavors, personal adventures, and ambitious ideas. Hang in there with me, I'm not done yet!

FOREWORD

—DR. MIKE MOSES, former Texas Commissioner of Education, Deputy Chancellor at Texas Tech University, Superintendent of Dallas ISD and other Texas public schools

DURING MY TIME IN PUBLIC EDUCATION, I HAVE HAD THE great pleasure of serving in several Texas school districts as a superintendent, at Texas Tech University as deputy chancellor, and for the Texas Education Agency as the commissioner of education. Throughout my career, I have had the opportunity to lead a variety of organizations of different sizes, serving diverse populations and with different goals.

One thing that was always a constant for me, no matter what organization I was leading, was using common sense in my decision-making. I have found that common sense is a universal language, and with it, one can be comfortable talking to a bus driver, a president of a university, or the governor of Texas.

I have followed Jim Largent's career since he was a young first-time superintendent in Nacogdoches County, the area where

I grew up, to his stops in Rusk and Granbury, where he retired. In this book, you will read tips, advice, and scenarios that place you in the seat of a superintendent, with ideas on how to handle a variety of situations and people from parents to board members. The book also includes a very good guide for advancing a career in educational leadership and how to devise a transition plan to ensure success.

This book will prove to be beneficial for new and aspiring leaders and others who just need some good counsel as they navigate the increasingly volatile role of being a school leader. In his book, Jim covers a lot of the intricacies of running a school district and many topics that leadership preparation programs do not cover.

I am proud to call Jim Largent a friend, and I know you will enjoy this book as much as I. Using these practical tips and advice will no doubt help you as you lead institutions that house our most precious resource, our children.

Introduction

WHAT THIS BOOK IS NOT

"Leaders become great, not because of their power, but because of their ability to empower others."

—JOHN MAXWELL

IF YOU BOUGHT THIS BOOK TO FIND THE LATEST psychoanalysis of educators or the latest think-tank-based theories of leadership, you are in the wrong place. As leadership theories have evolved over time, it seems a prevalence of people spout research, leadership models, the latest programs-in-a-box, and other ways to convince staff to follow them. There is a better way.

In this book, I share concepts, ideas, stories, and situations, and how I used them in my career. I also discuss how to work with a variety of people, from bus drivers to board members to irate parents. Finally, I share a series of commonsense steps and strategies that take leadership back to the bare bones of what actually works. You will find that leadership is effective if you just stick to very specific time-tested principles.

1

This book is meant to serve as a reference for leaders to turn to when needed. It also includes a bonus chapter that provides a blueprint for how to advance in a career in school administration, as well as how to transition into new jobs or opportunities. While written from the perspective of a superintendent, whose goal was once to *become* a superintendent, these commonsense concepts apply to virtually any leadership position in any organization.

As a disclaimer, I will say that this book especially details the nuances of working with departments and school finance, and some laws I cite are specifically based on my experience in Texas public schools. While I believe the common themes and suggestions I make will work in any state and in any school, some state or local laws might affect the execution.

I encourage you to read through the entire book once and then keep it around as a reference, sharing with colleagues to remind yourself and them of commonsense strategies that work. Hopefully this will be of assistance when you are bogged down with a lot of noise or maybe looking for ideas on how to handle certain situations. As a bonus, I have included an additional chapter that focuses on the job search, getting your foot in the door for potential jobs, interview tips, and how to develop a transition plan for success once the new position is attained.

Chapter One

WHY THE WORLD NEEDS COMMONSENSE LEADERSHIP NOW

"If your actions inspire others to dream more, learn more, do more, and become more, you are a leader."

—JOHN QUINCY ADAMS

WE LIVE IN A TIME OF CHAOS. OUR DAILY NEWS IS FILLED with stories of hate, violence, and tribalism, with people throwing lies and blame in all directions. And our schools have become targets of the same culture-war issues we see in society. I don't know of another time in our history, except maybe during integration, that schools have been so embroiled in politics as they are now.

Unfortunately, many people in positions of authority, elected officials, and influencers on television and social media are so adept at using dog-whistle tactics that their followers believe anything and everything they say. These influencers have such a stranglehold on their minions that facts don't matter anymore. If they say it, their followers take it as the gospel truth. This causes lots of problems for leaders, especially school administrators making decisions that affect a microcosm of society.

Most successful school leaders feel we can talk to, reason with, and come to some agreement with almost anybody. But there seems to be a growing segment of people in society who live in a fabricated world, and no amount of reasoning with them will matter. The tribalism in our country is out of control, and a large group of good people believes that false information written on social media sites by a loner in his mom's basement is more accurate than what is reported in reliable national news.

My goal here is to give school administrators some proven, time-tested strategies that work even in the midst of chaos. Nothing I write is rocket science, but I believe that in times like these, leaders should go back to the basics of leadership in running organizations. In fact, these commonsense strategies may be the only approach that will work in today's crazy world.

WHAT ABOUT CREDIBILITY?

Although I have a book, some published articles, and a dissertation on my resume, I am not one to try to place focus on myself for my schools' successes. I prefer to work behind the scenes, giving credit to those in the classrooms or on the field.

So, at this point, you may be asking, "What gives Jim Largent the credibility to tell me how to lead?" That is a great question, one I would ask if I were you. Let me give you a quick synopsis of my career and what I consider my leadership victories.

I spent thirty-one years in public education as a teacher, coach, athletic trainer, assistant principal, principal, and superintendent. My school boards nominated me four times as Texas Superintendent of the Year. I was never once fired, never asked to leave a job, always had my contract renewed, and was offered a raise every year to stay in my current position. Believe it or not, in today's volatile and sometimes toxic environment around schools, that in itself says I was doing something right!

As head coach, I took over a baseball team that had won only three games in the previous five years. In my first year, we won nine games, and in my second and third years, we went to the playoffs, once as the district runner-up and then as champion. In my final year, we went three rounds deep in the playoffs and lost a one-run decision to the eventual state finalist.

As a principal, I took over a school when the former principal left for a larger district. In four years, math scores rose by 38 percent, reading scores by 19 percent, and writing scores by 13 percent. In addition, the school reached a campus rating it had never achieved, and we achieved this rating four years in a row.

In my first stint as a superintendent, I was hired at Chireno Independent School District as the youngest superintendent in the state at the time. During my three and a half years there, we doubled the fund balance, successfully passed a bond issue with 82 percent of the vote, and were named a Title I Honor school and Commended school in subsequent years. When I left, the district was in great shape financially and academically, and morale was high.

In my second position as superintendent, I moved to Rusk ISD, a school seven times larger than Chireno, and remained there for eleven years. By using some of my strategies, we moved the district forward in all areas and again saw gains in academics, community engagement, facility improvements, and campus and district ratings. In one of my final years in Rusk, the local chamber of commerce named me Citizen of the Year.

My final stop as superintendent occurred in Granbury ISD, a school four times larger than Rusk, in the Dallas–Fort Worth area. GISD had just gone through a massive staff layoff due to being heavily overstaffed according to Texas Education Agency standards. Morale was low, there was much distrust between campus and central office staff, and staff gave horrible ratings to several departments in a survey done just prior to my arrival. In fact, while I researched the district as I prepared for my interview, several colleagues warned I would be taking a huge career risk by going there, due to the district's past problems.

In my six years as superintendent there, we reorganized the central office, replacing about half of the leadership team. Those who remained embraced my leadership style, refreshed with a new sense of freedom and ability to lead in a way that was best for campuses and departments. These personnel moves quickly improved morale and allowed us to improve key areas in the district.

Over those six years, we completely updated the facilities throughout the district. We updated every campus in some way, and we transformed a former campus into an open-concept administration building. At our high school, we built a 100,000-square-foot career and technical center that was state of the art at the time, and we started a mentor-led program that taught students to build fully functional airplanes!

Our high schools made *U.S. News & World Report*'s top 10 percent of campuses in the country, introduced project-based learning throughout the district, and received world recognition with our F1 in Schools program, which quickly became a perennial national champion, competing in the Middle East in world competitions.

If I were bragging about myself, the best thing I could say is this: I believe I left every place I worked better than it was when I arrived. That is not taking anything away from anybody I replaced, as I followed some very good leaders in most instances. But I think the goal of any leader should be to better the work environment. I honestly feel I did that, and I believe my coworkers would agree.

THE GOOD AND THE BAD

We can learn from good leaders and bad leaders, and in my career, I have seen many examples of both. I have worked in small, medium, and large schools and around a wide variety of leadership styles. I picked up on key concepts and areas of focus that made many good leaders. From others, I learned what *not* to do and observed how a leader's actions can negatively impact an entire organization.

Throughout the book, I've included "What I Learned from…" features to highlight some of my colleagues and mentors who taught me valuable lessons relevant to good leadership qualities.

WHAT I LEARNED FROM ED PEVETO: PEOPLE WANT TO BE LED!

Ed Peveto was my athletic director and head football coach at Coldspring-Oakhurst CISD. I knew of him when I was a student in high school, as my Kirbyville Wildcats were sometimes in the same district as Coach Peveto's Orangefield Bobcats. With my burning desire to be a head coach and the baseball program at Coldspring being at rock bottom at the time, he took a chance on me and tasked me with building a baseball program.

Ed was the kind of guy people from the outside loved to hate, but if you worked for him, you loved him. You probably know the type—bigger-than-life personality, loud, brash, confident. Ed was all of those, but there was no doubt about two things: 1) Ed loved being around kids and coaches. 2) Ed loved football, analyzing for hours every aspect of the game and his players to try to improve team performance.

I have never seen a guy with so much influence over a group of kids. I mean that in a good way. Ed took over a program in Coldspring that was loaded with talent but had lost direction and was not winning. Kids there were yearning to be successful and willing to do whatever it took to win.

Ed did little things to instill that positive influence he had over kids. When our team took a water break, the trainers had cups of water filled up and in a line. The players ran to the line of drinks and knelt in front of it. They didn't grab their cups until the coach instructed them to drink. At the end of practices, the team ran wind sprints and were always breathing heavily as they gathered around the coach for the last word of the day. One time, he yelled, "Quit breathing hard. You're not tired!" Immediately, the kids stopped their loud, labored panting and began to breathe normally.

The final thing I learned from Coach Peveto is that if you want to get the most out of people, you sometimes have to challenge them to do things that are uncomfortable. Ed put all his athletes through what he called boot camp. The process took several weeks but never ended until the kids had a "perfect day."

Boot camp was typically held in early spring, and no matter the weather, coaches and players wore shorts, T-shirts, shoes, and socks—nothing else. Now, most months in Texas are not brutally cold, but some days dip into the twenties or thirties, and on those days, it is no fun to be underdressed and dive through a hole full of freezing, muddy water or tackle other difficult obstacles for forty-five minutes! This was all a mental game for Coach Peveto to have his players prove to themselves that they could do more than they thought. People are hungry for leadership and will follow great leaders.

WHAT NOT TO DO

For all of the good leaders I have known, there are definitely some not-so-good ones, too. As most people know, sometimes you can learn as many don'ts as dos. Here are a couple of lessons I have learned from unsuccessful leaders:

You can't demand respect, trust, or loyalty. As much as some leaders would like to expect, you can't just walk into a new job and instantly demand respect, trust, and loyalty. They have to be earned! Yelling, making demands, and getting upset are all ways to quickly lose respect from your staff. While you garner a small amount of respect just by the position you hold, to be an effective leader, you have to earn the respect of your peers through respectable actions.

I have never seen a truly successful leader treat people badly. Everyone has a bad day and does or says things they regret, but leaders who consistently act irrationally, snap at staffers, publicly humiliate others, and generally are in it only for themselves never get the respect they so desperately desire.

Even though employees may smile and nod in these leaders' presence, in the background they are usually saying, "What a jerk." People who work for you should not feel they have to bring you things, gush over you when you walk in the room, or give you special treatment. If this is you, get over yourself—you are not that important!

Don't turn your nose up at the work. When I was a coach, one of the head coaches I worked for always took off immediately after football season to travel and go hunting. Combined with the Thanksgiving and Christmas holidays, the coaching staff rarely saw him until the New Year. He let his assistants do all the work and was nowhere to be found for a fairly lengthy period of time.

While I'm sure he had the blessing of the superintendent and may have even had this arrangement written into his contract, it was not a great way to build loyalty among staff. If you want to build trust and respect with people around you, you have to be in the trenches with them and not just be the guy calling the shots when fans are in the stands.

The leaders who influenced me the most share a common theme in that they all did things to make personal connections with their staff. They knew that building a team of staffers who trust and respect one another pays dividends in the future. In almost every case I have seen, when leaders don't spend a lot of time building teams with trust, their leadership is not effective and their tenure usually ends with a sudden crash.

Chapter Two

STAFFING IS NO LAUGHING MATTER

"Choose a job you love, and you will never have to work a day in your life."

—CONFUCIUS

I FIND THAT MOST PEOPLE JUST WANT TO BE TREATED fairly, get paid a fair wage, have a good work environment, and enjoy coming to work each day. Education is such a challenging livelihood that unless it is a calling or passion, some people will not enjoy the work. Those who feel uninspired will often be miserable, be less-than-ideal colleagues, and usually burn out and move on to other careers.

I have always been led by the following philosophy: *hire good people who are experts in their field, set expectations, and then get out of their way and support them as needed.* I truly believe this and have tried my best to do this with everyone I've worked with. Staffers need to feel confident in making independent decisions, and they should not have to worry about being overly monitored or reprimanded if they make a mistake.

With the right people in place, almost anything is possible.

OUTSTANDING TEACHERS

If you give me a great teacher with a drive for success, I could put them in a classroom with a pile of rocks and wooden blocks, and they will make sure their kids succeed. That is just the way it is with some teachers. They don't complain about what they don't have, or the makeup of their classroom, or the latest computer program they really need. They take the available resources and come up with amazing lessons that inspire their students to learn and enjoy being in the classroom. It is truly a gift, but for those teachers who have it, they really have it! If you can get the *people* part of education right, you are well on your way to leading a successful organization. Anytime I took a new job, during my first meeting with all the staff, typically at a first-of-the-year convocation, I conveyed this message: "As far as I am concerned, we only have two employee classifications in this district. Teachers and support staff." I wanted to make a very clear point that the teachers in our schools are the most important employees we have. They are on the front lines of delivering education to students. They are the tip of the spear, where the rubber meets the road, which often determines whether our students will thrive or suffer. In a school district, no employee is more important than a teacher, period!

After making that point, I went on to discuss how everyone else, from the bus drivers to the superintendent, is here to make sure the teachers can do their jobs with the least amount of stress, with strong and clear direction from leadership, in a clean and safe classroom filled with necessary supplies, and with all the support needed to do their jobs. The bus drivers need to make sure the kids arrive safely, cafeteria workers provide them with nutrition for the day, custodians make sure the classrooms are clean, and maintenance workers make sure everything is working and in order. All the departments in the central office exist to support teachers. There is not one department in a school that is not a support for teachers. None.

Now, with all that support comes a lot of responsibility and expectations. My goal as superintendent was to hire the best teachers possible, give them everything they needed to do their jobs, pay them as well as we could, and then expect them to perform. I prided myself on telling my teachers each year, "If you absolutely need something you don't have, let me know."

When teachers occasionally came to me with any feasible request, I made it happen. I did not want them to ever say, "If I only had 'such and such' I could have done a better job."

So, how do you best support the most important employees in your district? Administrators are severely outnumbered by staff, so it is virtually impossible to have a one-on-one relationship with each of them, especially in large districts. Teachers want to know that you, as an administrator, are in the trenches with them and not just sitting in your office on high looking down on the kingdom.

In almost every school I ever led, by the end of the first month or two on the job, I had teachers stop me in the hall to say, "I just want you to know that in two months, I have already seen you on our campus more than I saw the last superintendent in the past five years." Teachers want to see you, and they want to know you are interested.

WHAT I LEARNED FROM MELVIN HOUSTON: BUILD A FAMILY ATMOSPHERE WITH YOUR STAFF.

Melvin was the first athletic director I worked for out of college. He was the rare Black head coach in the piney woods of East Texas in the '70s and '80s. All who knew him respected him as a great leader, funny man, and one who did not see color. He raised a great family who grew up sharing his sentiments.

Melvin taught me the value of creating a family atmosphere in the workplace. Our coaching staff worked hard, truly enjoyed one another, and remained close friends outside of work. Our spouses were friends and spent time together when we were coaching. They traveled to games together and, after each home game, had a party at someone's house to socialize and laugh.

This was a great environment, and we had a lot of success in my time there. Melvin created that atmosphere because that is what he expected and how he lived his life. Only after I left did I fully appreciate the atmosphere in Woodville. My next position was with a staff that rarely socialized and had their own sets of friends outside of work, so it was definitely more of an isolated feeling and not nearly the family atmosphere Melvin created.

LEADERSHIP THEORY IN THE WORKPLACE DYNAMIC

This is the only section in which you will hear me talk about researched leadership theory. When I was working on my doctorate in education, we spent an entire course researching and discussing the different leadership theories at the time and coming up with our own. One type of theory stuck with me, and I used it as the basis of my leadership style throughout my career. There are various versions, but the general philosophy is that we have to lead employees differently based on their levels of professional maturity. Focusing on the ability and willingness of individual employees, it allows you to lead each person in a way that will get the best out of them. Leaders must adapt to employees based on their abilities and willingness. By knowing the strengths and weaknesses of individual employees, a leader can lead in a way that builds on their strengths and helps improve their weaknesses. We can generally place our employees in four different categories:

1. *I Can't Do It and Don't Want to Do It.* These employees are unable to do their job properly because they simply don't have the training or the will to do it. They need lots of one-on-one direction and almost need someone to prescribe exactly what to do and when to do it. These are the most difficult staffers to deal with because they don't want to improve or make any substantial contributions to the organization. These employees will either experience a complete shift in thinking and turn their performance around or, more likely, will leave the profession after being fired.

2. *I Don't Know How, but I'm Willing to Learn.* These employees are willing to do the job but simply don't have the skills necessary to do it properly. Typically, these are new employees who are overwhelmed with their new job but excited and motivated to do better. A good leader can make this employee a good one by supporting and coaching them and celebrating with them when they achieve success. Ultimately, these staffers take on additional responsibility and become more confident and productive at their jobs.

3. *I Can Do It, but I Just Don't Want To.* These employees have the skills necessary to do a great job but are unwilling to do so. Sometimes they have seen leaders come and go and are not willing to change, choosing to wait out the current leader for the next one. A leader working with these people needs to spend time providing feedback and support, asking the employee how they can help. These employees can sometimes be pot stirrers. They sit in the lounge and try to corrupt other employees with negative comments about everything from leadership to bad coffee. A leader must win these people over and get them on their team. Otherwise, these people can corrupt an entire organization if left unchecked.

4. *I Can Do It, and I Want To!* These are your best employees. They have the necessary skills for the job and are willing to jump in and do whatever it takes to make the organization successful. A leader should delegate to these people. Give them direction and then let them run with it. Provide input when needed, but otherwise, give them the autonomy they have earned. One caution is to not let them do everything. These employees often agree to

serve on every committee, sponsor every club, and do anything you ask of them. While you appreciate their willingness, this can cause them to burn out quickly, and they'll find themselves overwhelmed by all the duties and extras they have taken on. Do everything possible to make these people feel valued and loved, and continuously ask what you can do to make their work environment even better.

For me, this simple theory is the perfect commonsense model for leadership. It requires you to lead people a little differently based on where they are in their career, their confidence, their skillset, and their willingness to get on board with what you want to do as a leader.

Chapter Three

A SHOUT-OUT TO EFFECTIVE COMMUNICATION

"Leadership requires two things: a vision of the world that does not yet exist and the ability to communicate it."

—SIMON SINEK

COMMUNICATION CAN COME EASILY TO THOSE WHO HAVE innate leadership qualities, but it has to be deliberate and consistent. Personal interaction, email, social media, newsletters, billboards, texting, and group meetings are all effective ways to communicate with people. Choosing the best ways to communicate within your organization involves several factors, so ask yourself the following: Who is my audience? How large is my organization? To positively impact the most people, should my communication be seen, read, heard, or all of the above? Consider the various communication methods outlined here.

IN-PERSON INTERACTION

Unless written documentation is necessary, in my opinion, personal interaction is always the ideal way to communicate. Too many times, I have seen email chains, group text messaging, and other forms of communication go awry because someone misunderstood context or simply did not read the message thoroughly enough (or at all).

Your organization's size could dictate whether or not personal interaction can serve as a main form of communication. If you are leading a small campus with less than thirty employees, it may be very easy for you to personally communicate with employees. By simply making a point to see your employees each day, you are likely perceived as a great communicator.

Be at the school before your staff gets to work, greet them when they enter the building, and ask them about their family and how their week is going—anything to build an authentic rapport with staffers. Being visible in hallways, promptly checking on issues, and following up with problem students are also ways to establish an accessible communication style that lets staff know you are concerned for them and want them to feel supported.

As a superintendent, a strategy I used with much success was campus walks. Depending on the size of the district I was in at the time, I made a point to visit each campus a certain number of times per month. In the first very small district I worked in, I made it around the entire district several times a week. At the end of my career, when I was in a district with fifteen campuses, my goal was to visit each at least twice a month. I kept a spreadsheet, putting checkmarks as I visited each campus, to make sure I hit my goal.

These campus walks were casual and informal, not something I made a big deal of. I was not there to evaluate people, spotlight problems, or try to intimidate anyone. I made it known at convocation and new teacher inductions that this was just something I did and to not be alarmed when I walked into their classrooms unannounced. I wanted my interactions with teachers to be spontaneous and nothing they needed to prepare for. I wanted them to see that I was visible around the district and very interested in what was going on in their classrooms.

Now, I will say that on more than one occasion, I walked by a classroom where students were socializing and obviously not doing anything productive while the teacher sat at their desk on a computer or phone. I always went into those classes to ask what the kids were learning that day. It usually made for an uncomfortable conversation with the teacher, who had to come up with some excuse, knowing that they had just been caught loafing on the job. I never reported this to the school principal—unless it happened more than once. If so, I informed the principal that they may want to spend a little more time around that particular classroom to make sure what I saw did not become a common occurrence.

As an organization gets larger, especially those with hundreds or even thousands of employees, in-person communication can get tricky. But despite the size of your school or district, you should employ many additional methods of communication to effectively reach employees and constituents.

WEEKLY EMAIL MEMOS

One of the easiest-to-use modes of communication is simple email. I find that a weekly memo is one of the best ways to use email as a communication tool. In my final seventeen years as a superintendent, I sent out a memo every Friday during the school year. I called it the *Largent Weekly,* and I emailed it to every employee, board member, and substitute teacher. I can count on one hand the number of weeks I did not send out my memo. I normally sent my weekly out on Friday mornings before 10:00 a.m., and if for some reason it was delayed, people asked why they hadn't received it yet. That made it even more deliberate for me because I knew they expected and appreciated it. So, what was in my weekly that made it so special?

- **The first part of my weekly email was a brief description of my week**—what I did, who I saw, and maybe a bit of inspirational or morale-building words of wisdom. Employees are always interested in what their supervisor is doing, so by giving them a little window into my world, I think it helped them appreciate some aspects of my job.

- **Next, I had several bullet points of things I needed the staff to know.** It might be something I saw that needed to be addressed, a particular incident that I wanted everyone to know about, or a reference to a policy, law, or upcoming important date that I needed them to know about. These were not things that principals would cover in a staff meeting but things that they probably didn't know or needed reminding of.

- **I added a section called "Legislative Update,"** in which I gave a brief synopsis of what was going on in Austin's legislature and some key bills I was watching. While this was not partisan, I gave my staff factual information, such as how a local senator or state representative voted on a particular bill. This was also a good section to notify my staff about the importance of voting, let them know when the voting window was open, and encourage them to use their conference or lunch period to vote.

- **Next, I took the staff through an "e-book study."** I chose a book I thought would be pertinent for the year, and every week I summarized a chapter or two, highlighting the importance of that particular part of the book. Over the course of a school year, I covered an entire book, hitting its key points. This was a good way to complete a yearly book study.

- **After the book study, I included excerpts of emails I received throughout the week that praised staff members.** These came from community members, parents, or other staff members. I did not reveal the identities of the senders of the messages, instead simply stating this was from "a parent" or "a staff member," but I always placed in bold letters the name of the person being recognized. This was a way to give our staff accolades each week. Over time, as people realized what I was doing, I received at least five—and sometimes as many as twenty—emails praising staff members each week.

- At the end of each weekly memo, I closed with a motivational quote.

I didn't use any particular software or professional newsletter format to put together my weekly memo. My weekly was just a simple email with several regular sections clearly delineated by headings. It served as a great communication vehicle to reach my entire staff, and it was a way to consistently let them know the scope of what was going on in their world. My deliberate attempt to regularly communicate with them did not go unappreciated.

If you decide to do a weekly email memo, I offer this tip: each Monday, I started an email draft, which I saved, and as the week went on, I added content as something came to mind. This kept me from having to compose an entire weekly memo at one sitting. I just kept the draft open all week and added content as necessary.

SOCIAL MEDIA SAVVY

Social media has infiltrated all aspects of our lives. In many ways, it is a positive development—reconnecting with old friends, sharing vacation photos, keeping up with people hundreds of miles away. But an unsavory side of social media has become the norm for some—oftentimes anonymous—keyboard cowards. Some stir up controversy just by typing out a social media post filled with half-truths and outright lies that can cause immediate problems for school officials.

Today, it is almost imperative that every school district, campus, and program has some form of social media page that is constantly updated. By setting up some go-to social media sites and letting everyone know where to find them, you can amass a large number of followers who want to know every time you find something important enough to post.

A good communications team can keep the page up to date and fill it with positive stories about all the good things happening in our schools. But, maybe most importantly, social media pages can be used to dispel false rumors and put out factual information that people can immediately post and share.

One of my colleagues in a neighboring district was able to use social media to combat a mad employee. The employee had gone on social media to spout about why she had "quit" the school and how the school was a horrible place to work, and then she publicly bashed several employees. The superintendent responded with public documents proving the employee had been fired for lying on her application and failing to disclose past criminal behavior, to let community members know the former employee's posts were absolutely false. This online discussion ended with many pro-school comments, and the original poster disappeared from social media.

Perhaps one of the best uses of social media I have ever seen was by one of my principals in Granbury, Anna Roe, who livestreamed her morning walk-around on campus. Anna typically had a message for the day, popped in on a classroom or two, and used it as a way for parents and the community to see what was going on at school. This was a normal routine for her, and she amassed quite a following of people who regularly watched, posted comments about how awesome she was, or made generally positive statements about the great campus environment. This use of social media requires commitment, and not everyone can do it. But, for her, it was very popular, and the parents and others on campus appreciated her enthusiasm.

DATA DASHBOARD

In the early 2000s, the Texas Education Agency began releasing test score results and campus ratings in the fall each year. I was disgusted with how the state used test scores to pit schools against one another as well as label schools as good or bad. So, I devised a strategy.

Each year, during the same week the state released its ratings, we distributed a colorful, professionally produced flier titled "District Dashboard." Most years, we paid to place it in the local newspaper, and we also mailed it to the addresses of all students on file. We placed them at the chamber of commerce and gave them to every Realtor in town. These data dashboards quickly became a local Realtor's best marketing tool.

In this flier, we featured a data dump of issues people cared about. It included a graph that showcased our district's tax rate as compared to all the schools around us. We shared the number of students and staff, as well as staff-to-student ratios. In addition, we highlighted all of our campuses and what made each unique. We mentioned the colleges, universities, technical schools, and military academies recent graduates were attending, with lots of pictures of smiling kids.

This became a marketing tool for our district, and when people read something negative in the local newspaper about test scores, they immediately thought of that mailer they'd received that touted the school system's successes.

OLD-SCHOOL BILLBOARDS

Billboards serve as a communication tool that can be seen by anyone who happens to drive through your community. Billboards can be a way to advertise programs, brag on students or teachers, compete with private or charter schools, and tout pride for the entire school.

When I was superintendent in a rural area, we made a deal with a commercial sign company that allowed it to place billboards on a couple of pieces of property the school owned. In return, they provided us with year-round use of a billboard for free. We could change out the sign as many times as we wanted, and the sign company did all the artwork, printing, and hanging. It was a great deal!

We put up billboards to celebrate our sports teams, promote career and technical programs, and spotlight other student groups. But the most popular billboard in our small community was a huge picture of the senior class each spring to congratulate the students and wish them good luck. For the week or so after that billboard went up, every time I drove by, a car was parked on the side of the road as proud parents took pictures of their graduates.

After I moved to a larger district, we used billboards primarily for promotional reasons and to combat an influx of private and charter schools. Showing our community members the great things going on in our district helped build pride while also increasing the popularity of our schools and programs. Our best strategy was to rent as many billboards as we could around town, starting in July and lasting for a few months until school was well underway. With as many as eight to ten billboards rented at one time, we could showcase many different aspects of our schools. They featured photographs of students (with parental permission, of course) participating in science projects, sporting events, choir concerts, agricultural endeavors, and many other activities. We put our football schedule on one billboard, and some pithy messages on others. All of the billboards were branded with our district logo and school colors.

The above strategy began when a charter school and a couple of private schools started renting billboards in our community, attempting to draw kids from our schools to theirs. After seeing this, we used billboards in subsequent years to show everyone the benefits of public schools and to highlight the many programs we offered that the charter school in a strip mall or a private school with four teachers could never match. We never felt threatened by those alternative settings, and I'm sure our billboard campaign helped.

TEAM HUDDLES

One quick and effective method of communication is the use of huddles or team briefings. In football, a huddle is where all the players stand in a circle as the quarterback calls the play. In leadership, a quick huddle can get everyone on the same page. It is a way for a leader to go directly to their employees, have them join in an informal meeting area, and do a brief check-in or update for the week. It also provides time to ask the team if they need anything specific or if there is something the leader needs to know about.

This seems to be most effective when directors huddle with staff. A technology or curriculum director who is able to pull their staff together for a few minutes is a good example. Also, it is important during these huddles to stand in a circle so everyone can participate. By keeping everyone standing, it conveys to them that this is not a formal staff meeting that requires taking notes. If you have never incorporated a huddle or something similar, try it. Your staff might enjoy the briefings, and in a short amount of time, you can gauge its effectiveness.

STAFF SURVEYS

If you ever want to know how your staff feels about you or your institution, just ask! Periodically, I've surveyed staff, using a form they knew was anonymous and couldn't be traced. One year, I surveyed staff on my performance and that of my central office departments to get an idea of the general sentiment around the district. Another year, I sent out a survey asking campus staff to report on their school principals. My principals didn't necessarily like this, but I used it as a learning mechanism and never embarrassed my principals with the results. I shared results with them privately, and we worked on how to best address the survey results with their staff. All in all, we learned a lot through the simple use of a survey.

After I had been hired, but before I arrived, as superintendent in a particularly large school, the district conducted an all-staff survey of every department. I was not prepared for what I read!

It was clear from the terrible reviews that staffers were not happy at all with a few central office leaders and their departments.

"Unfriendly," "uncaring," and "unwilling to help" were recurring themes from staff. The results of this survey were disappointing, especially for a newly posted superintendent having to work with all these people. As I went over the results individually with my new staff members, some listened intently, were horrified by the results, and genuinely wanted to do whatever they could to turn things around. It was also evident that a few were not planning to change anything, made lame excuses for the survey results, and did not want my help in running "their" departments.

In the following years, when I reviewed survey results for principals, it was amazing that the findings basically laid out what a popular, successful, and effective principal should and should not do. The principals in our district who scored at the top of the list—and had test scores and morale to back them up—were deemed to be visible and personable, and they provided honest, frequent feedback. The principals who scored the worst with staff had almost exact opposite reports.

Teachers who rated their principal really highly had almost identical responses. Some of the most common statements that emerged in those surveys were as follows:

- My principal is visible, and I see them every morning when I arrive for work. They check in on me during the day to see if I need anything.

- My principal knows me personally and asks about my family and how I am doing on a personal level.

- My principal is interested in me more than just as a teacher.

- My principal is honest with me about ways I can improve, and my performance evaluation is a tool that helps me do better.

As you might imagine, when staff gave low ratings to their principals, the comments were very predictable:

- I never see my principal unless I go to their office.

- My principal never visits my classroom, and my students don't know who they are.

- My principal knows nothing about me or my family. There is no personal connection at all.

- I never know if my principal is on campus or not. They are not visible in the cafeteria, before school at duty stations, or walking the halls.

- My yearly evaluation is just a checklist, sometimes just put in my box. There is no conversation, no areas pointed out for improvement, and it really just seems like a task the principal has to do.

For those of you who are principals, the above illustration is a really good checklist for what your staff wants and needs from you. If you are a director or superintendent, these responses can give you clues about what key staff members want from you as well.

TEXT MESSAGING

Texting as a communication tool can be effective, but I think it is most appropriate for sharing information in small groups or for emergency notifications such as school closures or other after-hours decisions.

There are several phone apps that serve as hubs for group texts among students and staff. The best ones notify parents anytime a student is notified as a security measure to protect the district and teachers from false accusations. I don't recommend texting as a primary communication tool, and I definitely discourage its use between students and teachers or coaches, except for large group notifications.

HEAR THIS

Communication does not need to be a complex system. The key is to find what works best for you and your team, and then be deliberate about whatever method you choose. The worst thing you can do is announce to everyone how you are going to communicate and then do it only sporadically or change it regularly. Good, consistent, quality communication is an invaluable tool to use when leading any size organization. It is up to you to decide which is most appropriate and effective for your particular group.

PROFESSIONAL NETWORKING

Networking is one of the most powerful and important things you can do as a leader. Having regularly scheduled, confidential meetings with people in similar positions as yours will keep you current on latest trends, give you new ideas, and provide a confidential forum to run prospective concepts by trusted friends. You may be the only high school principal in your district, or if you are the superintendent, no one else in your community has the same job as you. Some people are quick to tell you what they would have done in any given situation, but until a person is in the leadership seat, they really don't know.

In my first year as a young high school principal, I formed a principals' study group for all the high school principals in surrounding areas. It started with just the principals in our sports and academic district, so about eight of us met monthly. We set ground rules that these meetings were confidential, so no one feared one of us would share stories from surrounding districts. We rotated meetings at one another's campuses, and even though many were rival schools, we all became friends.

As a new principal, I formed the group out of a desire to learn from older and wiser veterans. I think they appreciated that, and our sharing of ideas over the next few years was invaluable. These informal meetings became the basis for what I believe is the best means of personal development a leader can have—regular, consistent meetings with peers in an open-forum setting and in a trusting environment, where people can speak candidly, knowing that what they say will stay in the room.

STAFF MEETINGS

I believe it is also invaluable to have regular informal meetings with groups of staff members. As a high school principal, I devised a plan to meet with key staff on campus. We established a Monday "lunch bunch," and this proved to be a very important part of the success our campus experienced.

I formulated the group by dividing my entire staff by departments or job tasks. I sent out a ballot asking staff to vote on who they wanted to represent their department on the lunch bunch. A representative was appointed from each core academic area, athletics, fine arts, and auxiliary staff, and my counselor and assistant principal were involved as well. Representatives were not automatically made up of department heads, as I told the staff to vote for people who would speak up, be open, and best represent them on the committee.

After the committee was selected, we scheduled classes so group members would have the same lunch period. Part of the deal for being in the group was that they agreed to meet up during their lunch period one day each week. They brought their lunch, or on occasion, we provided lunch. The rules of the group were clear—open, honest discussion about what was *really* going on at the campus, what changes we could make to address any issues or problems, and how we could better the staff experience.

Over the next four years, our group met regularly and helped to significantly transform the campus into one that was high-performing, showed marked improvements in academics, and offered many more opportunities for students and staff. Much of our success was directly attributed to the discussions we held and the decisions we made in our lunch bunch meetings!

SUPPORT FOR SUPERINTENDENTS

When I became a superintendent, I was the youngest superintendent in our state at the time. I was green and in a job I had never held before. I was in dire need of a support group to help me navigate my new position.

Small rural schools often use cooperatives to share services with other schools. In this particular county, we had a special-education cooperative, of which several area schools were members. This co-op became one of the most valuable tools for my young superintendent career, and I looked forward to our monthly meetings so we could take care of the business of the co-op. More important for me was the time I got to spend with some grizzled veterans, who were key to my development as a superintendent.

After the normal feeling-out process a new member of a group has to go through, we all became close friends, and they served as a great mentor network for me. They were quick to give advice, and I was quick to ask questions about any of the plethora of department, tax, and budget issues I had never experienced before. They always gave me advice, told me who to call, and even came to my office on occasion to walk me through a new revenue calculation tool or show me how to maximize my budget estimates.

This group of mentors helped my development as a superintendent, and I owe them a debt of gratitude for taking me under their wings and helping me out in a nonjudgmental way. I have tried to do the same for other young superintendents, letting them know I am literally on call 24/7 if I can ever help.

SUPERINTENDENT'S STUDENT ADVISORY COMMITTEE

When I was a superintendent in smaller schools, I always felt I had a good connection with the students. I knew many of them personally and attended almost every school function. When I began working in a much larger district, I had to rethink my student engagement.

Acting on an idea I had learned from a friend in one of my networking sessions, I established a group of students to make up my Superintendent's Student Advisory Committee, or SSAC as we called it. I didn't want this committee to be made up of all the most popular kids or the smartest students, but instead I wanted this group to mirror the diversity of our school district. We had principals nominate students they felt were good representatives of the school and would speak out in a large group meeting. We obtained parental permission for them to serve on the committee, and we made sure to feed them each month, get their pictures on social media, and support and promote this group that helped me make healthy decisions for the district.

Over the course of the next few years, my SSAC was the first group outside my administrative cabinet to discuss issues such as a district-owned drug dog, expansion and renovation of our high school facilities, project-based learning, dress code and discipline issues, and the general morale and spirit at the high school. The group met with architects, police officers, and our curriculum staff to convey their thoughts. They served a vital role in transforming our school from an old, traditional high school to one that was modern and high-performing!

GROUPTHINK/SITE-BASED DECISION-MAKING

Years ago, some of the networking I now describe with staff and peers was called site-based decision-making (SBDM), and in recent years, "groupthink." I have always been a big fan of sitting down with smart people, hearing their ideas, and making decisions based on our collective thoughts. I think it creates buy-in and lets your staff know you are listening to them and want their input. When a group of smart people get in one room to openly discuss issues, you almost always come away with something you hadn't thought about or planned for. There are a few tips or methods to navigating groupthink.

I have seen organizations become hamstrung by relying so heavily on SBDM that the staff quickly begins to think no decision can be made without the committee's approval. I always made it clear in these meetings that I valued input and wanted to hear what staffers had to say, but final decisions, especially on personnel issues, were ultimately mine.

I used groupthink with any big decisions I made—bond issues, new curriculum, changes in the school day, calendars, and hiring key personnel. I never understood why a superintendent would hire a principal for a campus without including staff in the interview process. The same logic applies to a principal hiring a new teacher without getting input from department members and other key team members who will work with these people.

When consulting with a team for personnel decisions, I always wanted input from a well-rounded group of people who had no ties to any of the candidates. If I was hiring a new principal for a campus, I started by meeting with the entire staff to discuss issues they felt were important. I made it clear this was not a time to vent about the person who was leaving but that I was looking for positive, productive information for finding the right fit for the campus. After my staff meeting, I formulated a committee to be involved in the interview process.

A typical interview committee for hiring a new principal involved people from the central office, such as the CFO and curriculum director, someone from special education, a few key department heads or lead teachers, and at least one person in athletics or other cocurricular departments. These hiring committees might end up with just nine or ten people but were a good representation of the campus.

By having this variety of people on your committee, you accomplish several things. Each department can ask questions pertaining to their particular area of specialization. This allows them to gauge the applicant's support and knowledge of these programs. It gives everyone in the room a chance to hear about other programs and departments and about how the new leader plans to operate.

The most important reason, I believe, to use committees to hire new staff is to create a team of people who wants this person to succeed because they helped hire them and they are invested in their success. They can be ambassadors on the ground when staff questions them about the new hire. Superintendents and others who hire new staffers on their own, with no input from existing staff, unnecessarily open themselves up for scrutiny and at the same time do not give the new hire the best shake at success.

In one district where I worked, the superintendent hired all the principals by himself—no committee, no input, no rhyme or reason. He just showed up on campus and introduced the new principal! It is no wonder many of those leaders were not a good fit for the campus, and it created a revolving door of leaders moving through the district.

I made it very clear when using these committees that I had veto power, so if I was not comfortable with the group's top selection, I reserved the right to go to the next candidate. I remember this happening only once or twice out of the hundreds of people I was involved in hiring over the years, but it's important to set up that possibility with the group from the start. I was always clear that I wanted input, wanted questions answered, wanted a good discussion about the best fit for the position, but in the end, all of these people on our interview team would not be in the room with me if I had to fire this person. So, ultimately, it was my decision. By setting these parameters, it made the hiring process positive, and we almost always made the right choice.

FINAL THOUGHTS ON NETWORKING

No matter what position you are in, setting up a system of networks with peers is an integral part of success. By listening and learning from others, and applying what you hear to your decision-making, you eliminate the professional loneliness that can come from being the only person in your community doing your job. Having other professionals in your field validate your commitment or share ideas that have worked for them can stop mistakes before they happen or allow you to take shortcuts based on other people's experiences. Further, listening to students and staff is always enlightening and an important part of our jobs, keeping us connected to what goes on in the classroom.

Chapter Four

CULTURE CHANGE IN A COMMUNITY SET IN ITS WAYS

"The key to successful leadership is influence, not authority."

—KEN BLANCHARD

A SCHOOL'S CULTURE CAN CERTAINLY BE CHANGED relatively quickly with the right people in place and the right approach. However, a town's culture is almost impossible to change unless you have buy-in from key leaders across many different facets of your community.

I always slowly inserted myself into my new community. One easy thing to do that will create a bit of community buzz is to write personal cards to people who are helpful to you in your transition. Anytime I moved to a new area, I found people at prominent businesses and personally wrote cards to them and their supervisors. If a bank employee was particularly helpful setting up accounts, for example, I dropped a card in the mail to them. I also sent cards to the bank president and manager to let them know this particular employee is a great reflection of their business and that I enjoyed working with them. If you do this with several individuals around town, especially if they work for the power players, people will talk about the nice new school superintendent in town. While I enjoy doing this and am sincere in what I write in any personal note, there are definitely added benefits that come with being nice.

NOT OKAY...BUT GREAT

In one school district, I was told before I took the job that the people in this particular community were good people but generally not motivated to be great. Someone said to me, "They are okay just being okay." The school performance in academics and athletics, for instance, was okay but not spectacular. Throughout the community, some businesses in and around the downtown area were okay but nothing special.

As I began digging in and becoming more involved in the community, I found that the people there wanted to do great things but never felt motivated to take action. Most of the community leaders had held their positions for decades, and they seemed to like the status quo. There wasn't a lot of drama in town, as people just went about their routines. Nothing is particularly wrong with this attitude, but it is probably not the best if you want your community, schools, and businesses to keep up with growth trends and be successful. Years without progress can leave a community stagnant.

My approach was to let everyone know I wanted the best for our kids. Even though most of our students came from less privileged socioeconomic backgrounds, I constantly reiterated that they deserved to have just as many educational benefits as our wealthier neighbors in surrounding districts. While I couldn't put money in their pockets, I could provide an environment that made them feel special and worthy. New learning spaces, up-to-date technology, and facility upgrades soon followed.

We built a state-of-the-art performing arts auditorium with a competition stage, theater seating, and all the latest sound technology. Next, we upgraded our 1970s-era gym to a state-of-the-art coliseum with individual seating in a horseshoe arrangement that had a college-like feel. We also applied for—and received—grants that paid for one-to-one technology for most of our students. All of these elements over the course of several years raised the pride in our community as well as expectations from parents and community leaders. I believe our school district became the impetus for our community to improve.

Shortly after we completed our improvements in the school district, we saw local businesses update their buildings and business models. New businesses came to town, and we slowly grew better as a community. Our town took on a more modern feel, a certain pride was in the air, and people were no longer "okay being okay."

LAYING DOWN THE LAW

At another school where I was superintendent, I found that the school's relationship with local law enforcement was not good. The previous administration did not want police on campuses for fear it might shine a bad light on the school. If a student was caught stealing or with drugs on campus, the administration was told to keep it in house, handle it as a discipline issue, and not involve the police.

I had a completely different approach. My philosophy is that we are training our young people for the real world, so they need to know their poor decisions have consequences. I met with the police chief and local sheriff to express my views. Since there was a moderate drug problem at this school, I told the police that if we caught kids with drugs at school, I wanted them to be handcuffed and walked out of the school for everyone to see! I wanted to set a precedent that law enforcement would be visible at our schools, and if our kids made adult mistakes, they would be treated as adults.

When I discussed this with our law enforcement officials, I could see in their eyes that they were pleased at being asked to work in partnership with the school. After that meeting, I had the police chief's and sheriff's cell phone numbers, and anytime I called either of them, they showed up or sent an officer. We had a great relationship from that moment on, and the message to our kids and parents was apparent. I believe this relationship with law enforcement helped our school become a safer place.

COMMUNITY SERVICE

In one school where I worked, a middle school principal instituted a "day of service" on his campus. Student groups chose a charity or two and spent the day helping that organization. I liked the idea so much that we ramped it up to make it an annual school district event. Each year, we declared a day of service and included as many of our seven thousand students as we possibly could. Much planning went into deciding where students would go that day, and teachers, clubs, and teams lined up related activities.

We bought T-shirts for all of the staff and students who went out into our community for the day to help with nonprofits, charities, food banks, local small businesses, city and county agencies, and other organizations that needed help. Our students washed police cars and firetrucks, packed items for the local food bank, read to kids at daycare centers, cleaned area parks, decorated our town square for Christmas, and painted homes. Our town was flooded on this day with an army of staff and students all donning their red *GISD Serves* T-shirts. When people drove around town, they saw our kids helping in the community.

This event became well publicized, and our citizens got to see our students on a personal level. We helped many organizations and businesses complete tasks they could not afford to do or didn't have the manpower to accomplish with their normal employees or volunteers. What started at a campus was now a district-wide event everyone looked forward to. This was yet another way to help change the culture—and change the way many people in our community felt about our school and our students.

Sometimes, when dealing with the culture in a community, you have to take small victories when you can get them. Attending meetings with the "players" in town; forging relationships with law enforcement, bankers, the ministerial alliance, and other civic groups; being available to speak as requested; and generally being seen out in the community can all add up over time and pay dividends. By improving the culture in the community, everyone benefits in the long run.

RAPPORT WITH PARENTS

When it comes to students' parents, go into it with the assumption that the parents give us the best they have. They do the best they can with their current knowledge and capacity. I have never met anyone who wants to be a bad parent. A parent has never told me they raise their kids to be disrespectful, join a gang, do drugs, or fail classes.

Unfortunately, we can't control our students' home environments. We have no control over their home life, economic status, or family dynamics—including substance abuse—that may affect parenting styles, and we just don't know the whole picture of situations our students' parents are in.

We don't know if our students are being indoctrinated into a group of crazies who believe every conspiracy theory on the internet, or if their parents spend their days watching propaganda television and think all schools are communist-run organizations trying to feed their kids misinformation. If we go into any conversation with parents knowing these possibilities, we can at least start with a baseline and not be surprised if we run into some who have a deranged view of society.

THEIR KIDS, THEIR SCHOOLS, THEIR MONEY

At Lamar University, Dr. Bob Thompson hosted an annual Superintendent's Academy, which was a year-long symposium for up-and-coming superintendents. Attendance was invitation-only, and if you were nominated to attend the symposium, it was a big deal. We met once a month for a weekend conference at Lamar University, along with about thirty or so colleagues, and we spent a long weekend in New York at the IBM Training Facility. This year-long learning experience was a great setting to talk about concepts of leadership, learn new ideas, pick the brains of superintendents in attendance, and learn how to become a better leader in general.

One of the most significant aspects we learned and talked about was the concept of "their kids, their schools, their money" in reference to community members. Anytime you take a new job, you enter into an established culture. Research shows that the culture of a school or an organization can be changed fairly quickly using properly effective techniques, but changing the culture of an entire community is almost impossible. It can be done, but it is very difficult.

Dr. Thompson was trying to tell us as new superintendents to make sure the culture in a potential new job was the right fit for us and our families. Do as much research and ask as many questions as it takes to determine the culture you are entering before you take that new job. You can make all the right choices, hire the best people, and make great changes you know will work, but if the culture of the school and community is not a good fit for you, it may not end well.

If through the course of an interview, you find out the board members have a very different idea about the concept of school, think about that. I once interviewed with a school board that was obviously micromanaging the school on a daily basis. I let them know I couldn't operate that way but that if they were willing to change some procedures, I would love to come to their district. I soon found out that I would be expected to conform to their way of managing operations. I wasn't willing to do that, so I didn't make the move.

Always consider the intricacies of the job, the culture, the community, the makeup of the board and staff, and existing protocols and expectations in place before deciding if the job is right for you. Remember, at the end of the day, it's "their kids, their schools, and their money."

Chapter Five

THE DISH ON DEALING WITH DISCIPLINE

"Being positive in a negative situation is not naive. It's leadership."

—RALPH MARSTON

DISCIPLINE IS A PRIMARY ASPECT OF SCHOOL LEADERSHIP and one you will be asked about. Whether applying to be a teacher, an assistant principal, principal, or superintendent, at some point the interviewer will ask you about discipline.

SCOUT'S HONOR

At one point in my career, the new buzzword became "zero tolerance." Basically, this means that once the school rules are set, there is no room for common sense, listening to the student, or considering other factors. No, if a student does "x," the punishment is "y," no questions asked.

Shortly after the zero-tolerance policies went into place, I read a news story that went something like this: A student was expelled from a local high school because on Monday morning, the school found terrorist contraband in the trunk of his car. Another student had reported earlier to school authorities that his classmate had his trunk open before school and that he saw some disturbing items in the trunk. The student thought the school might be attacked that day. This immediately created a buzz around campus, as you might imagine. Police swarmed the parking lot, and all the school administrators were frantically trying to find the owner of the car, doing everything they could to prevent this impending school tragedy.

Once the police had the proper warrants and subpoenas to enter the car, they opened the trunk and found a large section of rope, a roll of duct tape, a pickaxe, a five-gallon bucket, a shovel, a machete, a number of random knives, and a backpack with food rations and bottled water.

The student who packed this contraband had to be a monster, right? He surely was planning to kidnap fellow students, tie them up with rope, bind them with duct tape, kill them with a machete, stab them with knives, and bury their bodies so they would never be found. Then he planned to escape into the wilderness and had enough rations to last several days. The school was lucky to have apprehended this terrorist before the damage was done!

After all of the contraband was confiscated, the car was impounded and the authorities located the student in his class-room. Police investigators began intense questioning, hoping to find his hit list of students he had planned to kill. They were not prepared for the answer they got from the student.

He was a straight-A honor student, had never been in trouble, came from a great family, and was by all accounts an all-American boy. He had been on survival training the weekend before to earn his Eagle Scout award from the Boy Scouts of America. His parents and local scoutmaster verified this. The student obviously had no ill intent, and his only mistake was leaving these items locked in the trunk of his car.

Yet, because this particular school had a zero-tolerance policy, authorities treated the student like a criminal and expelled him. A commonsense leader would have taken about three minutes to evaluate this situation and realize that no one at the school was ever in danger and that to punish the student this harshly was ludicrous.

BENDING THE RULES

I experienced a similar incident in a small country school where I was superintendent. A student was brought to the office because he had a 20-gauge shotgun and some shells in the back of his truck. It was another Monday morning, and it so happened to be just after the opening weekend of dove season.

Now, if you have never worked in rural schools, you may not know opening weekend of hunting seasons in Texas is a big deal! On the Friday before a big season, kids miss school or come to school with their trucks loaded and ready to go to dove, squirrel, or deer camp for the weekend. After a long weekend of hunting, it is entirely possible a student may forget to fully unload their truck before coming to school. Is this wrong? Of course it is. Is it against school rules? Sure. Is it potentially dangerous? Maybe.

But would common sense allow you to understand why this might happen and make adjustments to the rules? In this case, I said yes to bending the rules.

We treated the matter seriously, however, calling parents to retrieve the items and letting them know this could be serious. We made sure the student and his parents knew we were cutting him a real break and that this must never happen again. They were appreciative of our commonsense approach, the student learned a lesson, and no harm was done.

WHAT'S FAIR AND SQUARE?

Discipline is an area in which people are quick to offer opinions even if they know very little about the situation. One of the biggest complaints, even from school personnel, is that kids are treated differently from one another and that discipline is not fairly meted out. Some mention of this is on almost any survey of school staff or parents. The reason discipline often appears to be unfair is that every situation is different, and the students are different in each case.

Let's say two students are caught stealing items from a locker. Both students go to the office, and after the meeting, one student has in-school suspension for three days while the other is sent to an alternative school for three months. Not fair, huh? Well, what you don't know is that the student sent to the alternative school was caught stealing three previous times and the student with in-school suspension has a clean disciplinary record. Now does the punishment seem fair?

You also have to make clear that the rules are for everybody. When I was a first-year high school principal, I sent my superintendent's daughter home because her shorts were too short. I was just following our rules and treated her like any other student. As we were processing the paperwork for the infraction, several staff members asked me, "You do know whose daughter this is, don't you?" I smiled and affirmed that I was indeed aware.

Believe it or not, that one incident probably garnered more respect from my staff and students than anything else I did that year. My superintendent understood, too, and he respected me for doing the right thing. In fact, he used his daughter as an example when other issues came up at the high school, especially when parents thought their child was being treated differently. Several times, he told a parent, "He is not treating your child any differently than he did mine," using his daughter's ordeal as an example.

WHAT I LEARNED FROM JIM MARSH: PUT SYSTEMS IN PLACE FOR EXPECTATIONS.

When I was a coach in Coldspring, Jim Marsh was hired as our principal. Jim was friendly and really wanted to do a good job. He had replaced a very popular principal, but he had nothing to do with why he left, and he was just trying to do the best he could in a sticky situation. He had grand ideas and worked to establish student reward systems for behavior and academic success. He had some problems getting buy-in from the staff because we all liked the prior principal, but he came in with a positive attitude and slowly built trust.

About six weeks into the school year, our assistant principal left and never came back. At the time, I was the head baseball coach and athletic trainer and taught history classes at the high school. I was working on my master's degree at Sam Houston State University, and Jim knew this. He summoned me into his office one day and asked if I wanted to take on a new role as interim assistant principal.

As I was certainly planning to get into administration at some point, his offer intrigued me, and I quickly accepted. My "interim" tag was replaced when Jim went to bat for me with the superintendent, telling him I was doing a good job and that he didn't want to consider other candidates. For the next two school years, I was the assistant principal, head baseball coach, and athletic trainer at Coldspring-Oakhurst Jones High School. In addition, my wife, Jeri, and I traveled the hour-long drive to Huntsville a couple of days a week to finish our master's degrees at Sam Houston State. To say this was a busy time in our lives is an understatement.

As I had absolutely no experience in school administration, Jim was key to my development. He had me sit with him for an entire day as we brought in students one by one to discuss their misdeeds and what we were going to do to help them correct their behavior. After dealing with a few discipline issues, he would make a positive phone call to a parent or staff member, letting them know he was proud of the student or teacher. This added a little positivity to an otherwise not very positive task. After work-ing with several students, he sat back and allowed me to handle interactions for the rest of the day as he observed and made constructive comments to me after each student left the office.

Jim began putting in systems for student rewards. If the campus was kept clean, students who were not failing any classes had access to ping-pong tables and other games in the gym during tutorial time or lunch breaks. Over time, we saw a change in our student culture. Students picked up random trash in the hallway if they saw it, numbers of fail-ing students went down, and the personal responsibility and rewards systems began paying off.

Jim tasked me with creating an alternative setting for kids before they had to be expelled. This was well before the state mandated this practice. I also worked with Jody Cronin, our agriculture science teacher at the time, on integrating curric-ulum and doing cross-curricular work between departments and grade levels. We did things then that became popular, and even mandatory, years later.

For my first taste of school administration, I could not have asked for a better mentor than Jim Marsh. He worked with me, showed me the ropes, and put me in charge of endeavors that challenged me. He certainly prepared me for my first stint as a high school principal, and for that, I am grateful.

As a leader, I always tell people discipline is one of the easiest things to deal with at a school, and they are usually amazed when I say that. But in my experience, kids will do what is expected of them most of the time. And as school leaders, if we set expectations, the majority of our kids will do what we ask. When it comes to discipline, we end up spending too much time with a small fraction of students. By having procedures and expectations in place and a clear set of possible consequences, discipline does not have to be a horrible part of the job.

PARENTAL (OUT OF) CONTROLS

When dealing with school discipline, educators need to know up front that a parent is typically going to stand up for their child, especially when someone has accused the student of doing something the parent cannot believe the child would do.

As the new principal at a rural high school, I sometimes monitored areas outside the cafeteria. As I turned a corner to walk around the perimeter of the building, I happened upon Linda, who had a lit cigarette in her hand, smoke coming out of her nose and mouth. She was obviously "busted." As is normal, we went to my office, processed the paperwork, and assigned Linda to the appropriate consequence, most likely a few days of in-school suspension. I could tell she was unhappy, but I sent her on her way, and she was expected to start her suspension the following day.

Later that afternoon, I received a call from Linda's dad. He was irate over my accusation that his daughter had been smoking. I actually thought he was joking, having seen smoke coming from her nose and a cigarette in her hand. But the story Linda told her dad was that I had just thought she was smoking and, of course, that she was not a smoker. When I told her dad what I had seen with my own eyes, he said, "So, you are saying my daughter is a liar? My daughter will not lie to me—I know that for sure."

What do you say to that?

I said, "You know, I can tell you with 100 percent certainty that your daughter was smoking, and there are consequences that she will have to serve for that. How you handle that with her is your business, but I know what I saw." He finally hung up, mad at the world, thinking his beautiful daughter had been wronged and the school was "just picking on her again." The saying "blood is thicker than water" is certainly applicable here.

I came up with my own saying: "When a person's kids are involved, you can throw common sense out the window."

A CLOTHES CALL

In one of my first years as superintendent, an irate dad called me regarding his daughter, who had been sent home for a dress code violation. He was planning to come to the school to straighten us out about what his daughter would and would not wear. Since he was buying her clothes, he said, she could wear whatever he told her she could wear to school, and we couldn't do anything about it.

When I explained the school policy and the fact that she would have to follow the same rules as everyone else, he became even more incensed. "I'm about to come up there and whip some-body's ass," he said. I calmly invited him to come on up and said I would meet him at the door. He paused but then said, "I'm on my way right now."

About twenty minutes later, the door opened to my office build-ing, and I heard him tell my secretary he needed to see me and "get some things straight." My secretary called into my office and told me the dad was there to see me. My door was closed, so instead of asking her to let him in, I went to the door myself. My strategy was to let him know from the start that I was not intim-idated. I opened the door and made sure to get up really close to him when I shook his hand. After shaking his hand with confi-dence, I said, "Now, I understand you have some issues with our dress code." We began a lengthy conversation about schools, policies, why we have dress codes, and why we don't let parents decide what their kids wear to school. I listened to his position, and he and I actually had a mutually respectful conversation. So, the unhinged parent who was going to "whip my ass" became the guy who found out I am pretty reasonable. We had no more prob-lems with the dress code that year.

POINTERS FOR PLEASING AND APPEASING

In situations like the one above, the parent is usually trying to create a controversy with the person in authority rather than being concerned about the child's actions. This calls for a commonsense approach for dealing with parents who are being combative about school policy or other issues:

1) Let them talk and get it all out.

Many times, parents just want to vent and be heard. Other times, they are looking for an argument and the opportunity to walk away feeling like they've won somehow. My approach has always been to sit quietly with a notepad. I take notes on key points they bring up, I let them talk for as long as they want, and I don't interrupt. What I've found is that most of them don't have a whole lot to say, so when you let them have a voice, uninterrupted, they speak their peace in a very short amount of time. Then, you can redirect them to repeat the main points, making sure the facts are clear, and begin to explain the school's position on the issue. It is also helpful to show empathy, especially if you agree with some of their points.

2) Refuse to get in the ring with them.

As mentioned, some parents want a fight. They come into school offices mad as hornets, telling us how unfair administrators are and how they are not going to take it anymore. They claim they are going to call their lawyers, file suit, and make sure everybody involved in this horrible miscarriage of justice is fired! Some even get loud, use profanity, and make a scene.

Make it clear you are not going to fight with them. Professional educators do not partake in such nonsense. When a parent starts off a conversation by getting loud or using profanity, immediately redirect the conversation. Stop them mid-sentence and calmly say, "Whoa, now if you want to come into my office and have an adult conversation, I will try to help you. But I will not be yelled at, and I will not be cursed at. If that is your intention, then this meeting is over. Now, if you want to start over and have an adult conversation, as I said, I will try to help you."

Most of the time, this strategy provides for a reset and allows the meeting to continue smoothly. In the rare case in which a person is so belligerent they are out of control, I would first threaten to call the police. If that did not settle them down, we would call the police and issue the parent a no-trespass warning. I recall this happening only a couple of times during my thirty years in education, but it has happened. Some people just can't be reasoned with in a heated situation.

Chapter Six

COMMONSENSE CURRICULUM IS NOT A MYSTERY

"Leadership is learning to let go and really empowering people at all levels of the organization, and trusting them to do the right thing."

—SUNDAR PICHAI

WHEN I FIRST ENTERED THE CLASSROOM AS AN EDUCATOR in the late 1980s, I was given a thick world history textbook and was told to enjoy the year—ha! There was no curriculum training, no timeline, no scope, and no sequence. I just had to wing it. So, I did what any first-year teacher who had very little curriculum training would do. I looked through the book, picked out the sections I liked, and created some really good lessons on the parts of world history I knew about and was interested in. For the rest of the book, we just skimmed over the highlights.

If you were in Coach Largent's world history class in Woodville, Texas, in 1987, you learned a whole lot about early America, World

War II history, and Nazi Germany, but you learned very little about the Ming Dynasty or ancient Middle Eastern history. Sorry, kids! I was doing my best with the limited curriculum training I had, and my objective was to make learning fun and teach some important lessons. I think I accomplished that—although, by today's standards, I'm sure I didn't cover all the material I should have.

Some people make any discussion about school curriculum out to be some kind of mystery or secret. To me, curriculum is a simple concept. You have a grade level in elementary school or a subject in secondary schools, and you start with what a student should know when the school year is over. It's pretty simple. The trick is to determine how you, as a leader, ensure your teachers are teaching valuable lessons in the right sequence to get it done. This is where leadership comes into play.

A MIXED BAG OF GOODIES

If you google "school curriculum," you will get literally thousands of results. Everyone has their own magic potion that makes teaching easy, and all kids will learn the subject and master any tests given. Yeah, right! Not happening. When a teacher enters a classroom, they are walking into a room with students from all walks of life, different backgrounds, various styles of parenting, and varied base levels of learning. So, it's ludicrous to think you can walk into a class and teach every student the exact same way.

I always encouraged my staff to think of themselves as "education doctors." They would walk into a room each day with twenty-one "patients" who each needed a personalized prescription. Some just needed an aspirin once a day and they would be fine. Others needed emergency open-heart surgery! How to determine the prescription is the key. If you give aspirin to a patient who needs open-heart surgery, you are not going to like the results.

My strategy with any curriculum plan was to make it as simple as possible and give teachers as much freedom as possible. If kids were learning the material and proving that they had mastered what was required in third grade, or advanced calculus, I really didn't care how they got there. Some teachers have a gift of going into a room and figuring out the right prescription for all their kids, teaching them the material, and all is good in the world!

TEACHING TEACHERS WHAT TO TEACH

Others, like me in 1987, don't have a clue about how to sequence lessons, how much time to spend on a particular concept, or how to spread the curriculum out over the course of a year to ensure everything in the course is covered. These teachers need help by way of a curriculum model or plan. My perfect curriculum model was a plan that gave teachers a weekly guideline for what to cover as well as model lessons to help them decide how best to go about teaching the week's concept.

I also expected my staff to work together, especially those who taught the same grade level or subject matter. If Teacher A's students had 95 percent mastery on a particular concept and Teacher B's students had only 42 percent, I wanted Teacher B to consult with Teacher A about how they did it. By creating this collegiality, all students benefited, and it made all the teachers better. Now, many schools have gone to a Professional Learning Communities (PLC) model to accomplish this goal.

A curriculum model in Texas in the early 2000s, developed by teachers and sold to schools from service centers, set out to do just that. It had a year-long sequence of model lessons and timelines for each grade level and core subjects and was a really good base curriculum, especially for new or struggling teachers. It provided a guideline so that a brand-new teacher could walk into a classroom, follow the curriculum, and be sure they were teaching what the course required.

Unfortunately, during the era of political theater, this curriculum got caught in the "schools are trying to indoctrinate our kids" nonsense, and in some schools where the curriculum was mandatory, it became a public issue. Claims from politicians and political activists were predictably filled with lies and misinformation. Eventually, the state government banned schools from using the curriculum to appease its political base.

When I was the superintendent in a larger school and had a full staff of curriculum-focused professionals, we created a curriculum I thought was ideal. We had a sequence to follow, vetted lessons that were proven effective, and suggested benchmarks along the way. Then, we developed benchmark testing constructed at the district level. These tests were administered several times a year as a way to check on progress throughout the district, so we could monitor how all our schools were doing on the same concepts. This allowed us to drill down using data to guide teachers, grade levels, subjects, and campuses that were underperforming.

The final and most important piece of this program was that it was in a constant state of change. As newer, better, more effective lessons were discovered or brought to us by teachers, they replaced older, less effective lessons. Our curriculum document was an ever-changing tool for our staff. It was a great system and one I recommend if you have the curriculum staff to do it thoroughly and correctly. If not, curriculum companies have developed similar systems for purchase, and with the right evaluation, you can ensure they meet the needs of your school and state.

Curriculum shouldn't be the great mystery some make it out to be. Teachers and administrators should ask simply, "What needs to be taught, what is the best sequence for doing so, and what are the best lessons to ensure my students are learning?" By working with colleagues, consistently improving on vetted lessons, and ensuring that the curriculum meets requirements of the grade level or subject, teachers should welcome a curriculum program or document and use it as an invaluable part of their success.

TESTING AND ACCOUNTABILITY

Over the years, my attitude and thoughts about testing have evolved. When I became a principal in the mid-'90s, testing was not administered to every grade level, students weren't tested in every subject, and the tests were designed to let us know where we were as it related to students being on track with their peers. It was a great tool to measure the growth of individual students as well as to compare cohorts of students' progress from one grade level to the next. As a principal, seeing campus scores move up significantly is a sign your leadership is working, teachers are focusing on the curriculum, and students are excelling.

In my experience, this was when Texas had a commissioner of education, Dr. Mike Moses, who was a former public school superintendent and felt the Texas Education Agency was a governing body that existed to support local schools. Over time, unfortunately, many state agencies have reverted to becoming enforcement bodies filled with political appointees and policy wonks who have never worked one day in a school. It seems their sole purpose is to act as watchdogs or draft lists of rules and regulations that are nearly impossible to follow.

There are lots of dirty little secrets about testing that most casual observers, staff members, parents, reporters, and even most politicians don't know. In recent years, it was found that students were taking tests not even written on their grade level. It was discovered that the third-grade reading test was written on a fifth-grade reading level. How valid is a test result when the questions are written at a level the student cannot realistically be expected to comprehend?

The state has also begun embedding questions into tests to determine if elementary school children are on track to be "college and career ready." As I have said many times, when my kids were in third grade, I just wanted to make sure they were at least on a third-grade level. If they were higher than that, great! Trying to make assumptions for college based on a third-grade test question is ridiculous, in my opinion, and only complicates the data. I find it infuriating the depths to which our government agencies have gone to complicate what should be a simple process.

Common sense says you should expect teachers to teach a certain curriculum for whatever grade level or subject they are teaching. They should do assessments throughout the year to make sure students are on track, and provide additional guidance if they are not. At some point toward the end of the year, a comprehensive test should be given to let educators know if the student mastered the material for the year or not. Why not make 90 or above a great score, 70 or above satisfactory, and anything under 60 a failure? This would be so easy to do and even easier to understand, and it gives a real baseline.

EXTRACURRICULAR AND COCURRICULAR ACTIVITIES

On a less academic note, there are so many extracurricular and cocurricular activities related to schools these days that it is impossible to address each one. And while these activities aren't typically monitored as closely as academic curricula, it is important to discuss these groups, teams, clubs, boosters, and so on, because they can shine a good, or sometimes bad, light on your school any given year. I have found that these activities are an essential part of offering students a well-rounded school experience and can become crucial components of successful schools.

Extracurricular is any activity that is not tied to an academic subject. Sports teams, student clubs, and groups that focus on hobbies fall under the extracurricular category. These activities are "in addition to" the curriculum of a school.

Cocurricular groups take part in activities that are an extension of the classroom curriculum. Band, Spanish club, 4-H, and many others are seen as an extension of the classroom and are thus considered cocurricular.

I believe a successful school has a wide variety of activities available to its students. In my opinion, a well-rounded school has opportunities that touch on a plethora of student interests and allow students to find groups where they fit in, share common interests, and can focus on their favorites. Some students who feel out of place in school tend to shine in these activities outside the classroom.

When I taught physical education, I tried to do alternate activities to hit a variety of interests. It never fails that some sports make superstars out of students who otherwise do not show much athletic ability. When I taught archery, for example, it always seemed a student or two—who may not have been the best football or basketball players—came alive when I put a bow in their hands! The same can be said for yearbook staff, art club, jazz band, school choir, and the many other activities and opportunities that make up a successful school.

While giving students opportunities is great, be wary of some potential pitfalls as you manage your school's activities. Unfortunately, most revolve around money and the abuse of money by the adults in charge or by the volunteers who handle money. Even though these are volunteer groups, it is the school administration's responsibility to monitor their activities, make sure they follow school policies, and do annual audits to ensure finances are in order.

The best advice for any of these groups, as related to money, is that any money raised through fundraisers should be used to benefit the students, period. Many small clubs don't have much of a revenue source, so the potential for theft is very small. But some fundraisers raise tens of thousands of dollars, and these dollars must be accounted for.

Do a quick internet search for booster club theft, and you will see hundreds of articles about group sponsors using student activity dollars to bankroll their personal checking accounts. Many such schemes go on for years because the people behind them are well-respected and trusted parents who are always involved and volunteer to do everything. These people are often given carte blanche to use the club checking account or debit card to buy supplies, and when wrongdoing is finally uncovered, it is found that they bought gift cards, food, gas, and more with the funds from the club. In their mind, they feel justified because of all the hard work they do. In reality, they are committing theft of public funds, a serious crime.

Unfortunately, I have seen school employees, band directors, and coaches use these groups as personal slush funds to purchase very questionable items. It is important to have policies in place that specifically cover the purchase of automobiles, trailers, and a variety of other items that become the school's responsibility to take care of if not handled correctly.

I know of a coach who wanted to host summer camps for kids. Administrators agreed that he could use school facilities in the summer for no charge and keep whatever money he made off his camps as a supplement to his salary. In the coming years, his camps became so popular that he made more money from his camps than his teaching salary. I'm not saying this agreement was illegal, as school officials knew about it and approved it. However, this is an example of the need for implementation of policies and procedures to handle these situations. When information came out about how much money the coach was making off his camps without any expense for the use of facilities, it became an issue in the town.

Extracurricular and cocurricular programs are crucial parts of any school. But these groups should be subject to close scrutiny. Have a clear set of policies and procedures for handling money and getting approval for purchases, especially acquisition of property that might fall on the district to maintain or own. Keep the focus on what is best for students, and many of these issues will take care of themselves. Unfortunately, if allowed to go unchecked, egos and greed can cast a huge shadow on fortuitous programs.

WHAT I LEARNED FROM CHESTER JUROSKA: HIRE TALENT, NOT EXPERIENCE.

When I met Dr. Chester Juroska, I was applying for the high school principal job at Queen City High School in Northeast Texas. I went through the application process, and I could tell during the interview that Dr. Juroska liked my presentation. Afterward, he followed me out the door and told me I should probably start thinking about moving. He said that while he had a few more interviews to complete, he thought I was the guy for the job.

Sure enough, a day or so later, I was offered the position of high school principal. Dr. Juroska was different from any other leader I had ever worked for. He was high-strung and enthusiastic, loved the school business, and wanted to compete and win at everything from academics to athletics to cocurricular activities. His drive to win and compete matched up well with mine, so we hit it off immediately.

A few key things I learned from Chester are as follows:

Hire talent, not tenure. No one should expect that it is their turn for a position based on job seniority only. Being at a workplace for a long time does not automatically make you the best candidate for a job opening. Having the passion, ideas, and drive to succeed are much more important than time spent in a district.

Push the envelope. Don't ask the government for permission to do things out of the box. Do what you think is right for kids, and worry about government nonsense later. I see far too many leaders constantly worried about what TEA, the legislature, or some other government agency may think about activities that are progressive and forward-thinking but not of the norm. I wholeheartedly agree with Chester's philosophy to do what you think is right for your students and answer questions later if necessary.

Prepare future leaders. Dr. Juroska wanted to groom his administrators for their next job. He allowed me to be involved in all aspects of the school, even in areas where I had little to no authority. This allowed me to witness many ordeals a superintendent goes through and helped me tremendously as I prepared for my first superintendent position a few years later.

Chester felt his job was to prepare future superintendents and give them every opportunity to be successful. Because of his attitude and drive, he has quite an impressive list of people who became superintendents after working under his tutelage at some point in their careers. I owe much of my preparation to becoming a superintendent to Dr. Juroska.

Chapter Seven

PARENTS HAVE OPTIONS FOR A CHILD'S EDUCATION

IT IS PROBABLY QUITE CLEAR THAT I AM AN UNAPOLOGETIC supporter of public education. It is the system that is afforded every student in America, and students cannot be turned away from a public school based on the color of their skin, the financial status of their family, their political beliefs, or what religion they follow. It is also the system that grants every student the opportunity to better themselves, achieve their potential, and live their American dream.

Despite my belief that public schools are the best option for most students, I understand there are circumstances that motivate parents to look for alternatives to traditional public schools for their children. The reasons parents list for opting out of free public education are many, but most seem to revolve around religion, status in the community, or the belief that the local public school doesn't offer the quality education they expect for their children.

Because of the fact that more parents are choosing alternative school settings, it is important to explore today's primary options. Following is my take on various alternative methods of education for students.

PRIVATE SCHOOLS

I want to be very clear that I am not against private schools. If parents choose, for whatever reason, to forgo the free public education in their community and pay for private school, more power to them. Many parents, for religious reasons or because of a certain set of philosophies, friends, or activities, decide private school is best for their children. While I could, and have, debated the merits of that thinking, I respect parents' right to make that decision. Many great private schools do a wonderful job educating students.

I have very strong feelings regarding private schools, however, when politicians and activist groups introduce and support laws that allow public taxpayer dollars to subsidize private school education. On the surface, you might wonder why I would be so strongly opposed to this concept. So, let me explain.

Every person reading this book pays taxes. All of you pay taxes to a local city, county, or state, plus taxes on almost everything you purchase. In my city, we have a local park system, walking trails, ballparks, a skateboard park, a dog-walking park, and many other services paid for with my tax dollars. Taxpayer dollars are pooled together, and those dollars are used to make up the city and county budgets that pay for these services.

What do you think the response would be if I showed up to the city council and said the following? "I appreciate all the things you offer me in the city. But I never use the city parks, don't ride a skateboard, and have no need for ballparks anymore. So, take the tax dollars I pay for services I don't use and give me a voucher for my country club dues at our local private golf course." How do you think that conversation would go? The city council would laugh me out of their chambers and label me a nut for even suggesting something so ridiculous—and rightly so. But every time state legislatures across the country meet, a group of politicians proposes a similar scenario. They ask for tax dollars meant for public schools to be paid toward private education instead. And somehow, under these circumstances, it is expected to be taken seriously.

I could write an entire book on all the reasons this is a bad idea, but I am going to condense my thoughts here. In the public school system, students who live in a school district are guaranteed admission to their local public school. In fact, the Texas Constitution clearly states that the legislature of our state will "make suitable provisions for the support and maintenance of an efficient system of public free schools." In spite of race, religion, household income, language, or disability, you are welcome in public schools. The public school is required by law to admit you.

The typical private school, on the other hand, has a very detailed list of requirements students must meet in order to attend. Some only accept English-speaking students. Some cannot accommodate students with disabilities and don't offer services such as speech, physical, or occupational therapy. Many require a certain household income. Others don't offer transportation to or from school, so if you can't get to school, you are out of luck. Without going into further detail, you can still see that private schools create a set of guidelines that allows them to admit only the children who fall within a certain demographic.

For instance, if I wanted to create an "Ivy League prep school," I could. I would have admission requirements that set a threshold on taking a battery of pre-college admission tests or other baseline requirements that would eliminate students who might struggle academically. I could have an English-only policy, which would eliminate students from diverse backgrounds or who recently emigrated to the country and don't speak the language. I could even have a requirement that in order to remain enrolled in my school, every student must attend a religious service of my choosing each day. Then, I could offer "country club" sports—golf, tennis, and swimming—to further drill down the type of student I want to attend my school.

Do you see how easy it can be to manipulate admission requirements to build a school with very little diversity? Now, while my school would be full of high performers, there is no way I could compare my school to a public school. My school would be made up of a completely and purposefully selected student body, something a public school cannot do. And with the difference in clientele, the results are predictable.

A lot of politicians are perfectly fine with this. They believe that allowing parents to receive a voucher from their local school district to pay for private school is a great idea. In their fiery speeches demanding this, politicians and activists say it will allow less privileged inner-city students the same opportunities as everyone else. *Baloney!* What if the voucher from your local school is only $4,000 per year, but the annual tuition to your selected private school is $30,000?

Private school vouchers were never intended to benefit poor inner-city students. That is just more political fodder that makes the real motive come off as more acceptable. If politicians and private-school enthusiasts really want to help inner-city kids attend private schools, they should engage their wealthy benefactors, who provide billions of dollars in political donations and charity each year, to fund programs that fully pay for these kids' education—or, better yet, provide more resources to their local public schools so all students in the area benefit. Why is this not the focus?

In the end, this is yet another scheme to segregate students into two groups: those who can't afford a private education and those who can. Parents who would receive the vouchers are also those who are normally listed as campaign contributors to the politicians who push this concept. Coincidence? I think not!

CHARTER SCHOOLS

I was a high school principal in the mid-'90s when I began to hear about charter schools. Back then, it seemed reasonable, and I was excited about the idea. Charter schools were meant to focus on at-risk students who did not perform well in traditional public schools. They were an alternative setting that might be the key to these students' success. They were to be "labs of innovation," places where schools had the freedom to change curriculum, have nontraditional school days, hire nontraditional teachers, and incorporate other strategies that might reach the at-risk students they were targeting.

Some charter schools were structured like summer camps, located in off-the-map locations, with unconventional school settings and a variety of teaching methods. For students who struggle, have social issues, or don't function well in large crowded schools, this seemed like a perfect opportunity. One of my colleagues actually took a job in a charter startup and spent more than a year developing the curriculum. We talked about the developing curriculum and learning environments, and it sounded like a fun and exciting way to teach and learn.

Unfortunately, over time, what we have seen with charter schools is a money grab by politicians and businesspeople who have found a way to get taxpayer dollars and still call themselves a "public school." The fact is that these charters are taking local taxpayer dollars that could be used to enhance existing public schools in the community. In many of these schools, the focus is not on helping at-risk kids or those who don't fit in with societal norms. It is about revenue—making money for the charter school company. The corruption is ridiculous, yet some states, like Texas, continue to approve even more charters.

There are a couple of famous examples. In one, a state education agency gave a charter to a local NFL star, who basically opened a school for football and basketball. Fully funded by the state, this school was closed under a cloud of controversy almost as soon as it opened. Test scores were horrible, millions of dollars of computers bought with taxpayer dollars were missing (read: stolen), and the school was shuttered mid-year, leaving parents wondering where to send their kids to school. Of course, the local public school welcomed them back, and they returned to a normal routine, but millions of taxpayer dollars were wasted on this bad experiment. Countless examples of this are happening, but this one got more attention due to the NFL star being associated with it.

Another very public example focused on a large charter company found to be using taxpayer dollars to allow its executives to fly in private jets, rent out suites at professional sporting events, and draw exorbitant salaries while filling advisory boards and leadership positions with unqualified family members. When questioned by the media through the Public Information Act, these schools refused to release records, claiming they were a private business.

While certainly some charters do good work, traditional public schools beat charters in almost every category—attendance, graduation rates, test scores, college admissions, and more. You will be hard-pressed to find one category in which a charter school outperforms a public school in the same area.

HOMESCHOOLING

Homeschooling has been around for a long time but is becoming more popular, particularly after so many parents had to become home educators during the COVID-19 pandemic. With politicians promising vouchers, scholarships, or tax credits to allow parents to pay for their homeschool equipment, computers, materials, and software programs, there has been a big push to allow parents to homeschool their kids while the government pays for it with tax dollars. Some parents have used "homeschooling" as a way to take their kids out of public schools without violating compensatory education laws. Unfortunately, when parents do this because they are mad at their local school system, it almost always ends up with the children suffering. When they predictably return to public school, they are grade levels behind their peers and sometimes never recover academically.

During the pandemic, virtual and homeschooling took a big hit as the results from students staying home with parents resulted in horrendous test scores, a lack of learning, and serious academic regression for many students. As expected, this forced experiment proved beyond a shadow of a doubt that in-person education with certified teachers is by far the best method of delivering instruction to the vast majority of students.

To be honest, I have seen very few parents who are qualified to successfully homeschool their children. I know I couldn't have done it, and I have a doctorate degree in education. I have seen a few parents successfully pull it off. They were not mad at the local schools, but normally one of the parents was highly educated and took on the challenge of providing a well-rounded education. They studied geology, for example, then went hiking in a national park to see firsthand what they had learned. They wrote books and visited museums, and the parent was a full partner in the child's education. In reality, aside from a lack of social interaction, these students got a great education, and most of the ones I knew did very well in college. But the parents who are willing to go through this process and have the means and determination to do it right are few and far between.

I will tell anyone contemplating homeschooling their kids to spend a good amount of time working on social skills. Having your children around you all day, every day, is not a good way to teach them to interact with others who don't look, act, or think exactly like you. Successful homeschoolers get involved in youth league sports, church groups, or a homeschool network of other kids their age.

Homeschooling parents who don't allow their kid to be a kid are often faced with a child who lacks communication skills, becomes extremely introverted, and does not function well in social situations. As much as we would like to insulate our children from bad things in the world, this is one of the many reasons I advocate so much for public education. Our public schools are microcosms of the reality these kids will have to face when they reach adulthood. By trying to keep them isolated from controversy, diverse backgrounds, and negative influences, parents actually fail to prepare their kids for real life.

Chapter Eight

IT TAKES A TEAM OF EIGHT TO BE GREAT

"Nearly all men can stand adversity, but if you want to test a man's character, give him power."

—ABRAHAM LINCOLN

I WROTE MY DOCTORAL DISSERTATION ON SUPERINTENDENT tenure and the characteristics and reasons superintendents had for staying in one district for an extended period of time. A significant finding of my study was the effect a school board has on a superintendent's tenure. In fact, the two top reasons a superintendent leaves a district are for more money or to end a poor relationship with the school board—typically a group of seven elected or appointed board members. This group of seven board members plus the superintendent is often called the "Team of Eight."

In one of my early years as a superintendent, one board member had ridiculously unrealistic expectations of our sports teams, particularly basketball. His son, who was an average athlete, was on the team. As a former coach, I've spent a lot of time around high school and college athletics and have seen lots of ball games in my day. It is fairly easy for me to gauge talent level on the court, the level of coaching, and the potential for success. This particular team was not very talented. Only a couple of players could have even made the team in the next division larger than ours—nowhere close to a playoff-caliber team.

Anytime a better team in our area played us, we predictably got beaten badly. Unfortunately, this happened frequently. As hard as our kids played and tried to win, they were just not talented enough on the basketball court. Our opponents were quicker and faster, were better shooters, had more experience, and simply outclassed our kids athletically. But no matter how good the other team was or how badly they beat us, this particular board member always called me or talked to me after the ball game to rant about bad coaching and how we should have won. I tried to diplomatically reason with him, but he was concerned only with firing the coach.

Board members can be a superintendent's biggest source of support, or they can be an obstacle to moving a district forward. I've dealt with a wide variety of board members in my long career as a superintendent. First, let's establish that school board members are volunteers. They subject themselves to public ridicule, outbursts by constituents, scrutiny, and sometimes even vile treatment from their friends and community members. I don't want to discount this fact. Board members serve a vital role in our schools, and when they take the job seriously and follow the guidelines, they are a great help in moving a district forward. But some of the worst, if well-meaning, board members can cause detriment to the entire school.

TRUE PROFESSIONALISM

If we could all choose our board members, we would appoint those who exhibit professionalism. They genuinely love schools, kids, and school staff, and with all sincerity want to help make the schools in their community the best they can be. They are nonpartisan and don't run as a "true conservative" or a "progressive" candidate, understanding that a board member should be there for all children and not to espouse political beliefs.

The best of them have specific talents in a particular area. Maybe they are finance people, work in human resources, or have experience in the construction or maintenance field. Some might be college professors or retired educators. Others are stay-at-home moms who volunteer in the community and have a good idea about the pulse of the community buzz on a variety of topics. These board members are eager to give their opinions. They only want what is best for the school and its employees and are willing to help in any way they can.

ONE-TRICK PONY

Some people run to be on the school board for only one reason—they don't like a coach, a principal, or superintendent, and they want to get elected so they can fire that person and hire someone else. That is their only motivation for running for this elected office.

Most times, once these people are elected, they realize how the school board structure actually works, and they quickly find out they don't have hiring and firing authority. They either lose interest, serve their one term, and don't run again or discover they like being on the board and become a good member. In the worst-case scenario, a weak superintendent allows these people to pressure them into firing people who do not deserve it, beginning a cycle of turning the school board into a detriment to the district's progress.

HOLDING A GRUDGE

Occasionally, similar to the one-trick pony, a person runs for the board because they have a grudge against someone. I have seen this happen. A teacher or administrator is fired or forced out of a job they love and then runs for the school board with the purpose of firing the person they feel wronged them. I have also seen former principals or central office staff run for the school board in an attempt to "fix" all the problems they saw when working inside the district. Sometimes these people end up being good board members, but oftentimes their behavior as a board member reinforces why they were fired.

POWER HUNGRY

Possibly the worst group of board members are those who are power hungry. In my experience, the typical profile is that these people were never in a position of leadership growing up. They were likely bullied as a child or were the last to be picked for teams at recess, and as a school board member, they believe they now have some sort of power they never had, and by God, they are going to use it!

These people quickly forget about board policies and all the warnings of board micromanagement. They believe this is a time to flex their muscles, take power, and become the bullies they so despised in childhood. It normally begins with constant requests to be involved in decisions board members should not be involved in—hiring personnel, evaluating staff, and making campus decisions. Soon, their requests become demands that no decisions are made without their approval. In the worst-case scenario, a superintendent falls into this trap and allows these board members to take over the district. This can lead to the beginning of a total collapse of the organization.

I've known several board members who fit this profile, and in almost every instance, I could visit with them about it. We would discuss the role of a board member and the precedent they were setting for future board members, and then normally they would back off. As superintendent in a new district, in the executive session at my first board meeting, the board president said, "Jim, the board would like to meet each month in executive session for a short time without you in the room. We just think this will be a good time to let us talk about what is going on in the community and get us all on the same page."

Since I was their new superintendent, new to the community, and certainly not wanting to get off on the wrong foot with my new board, I could have just said, "Sure." But I knew if I did that, I would be setting a precedent that I could not reverse. I would look weak to my administrative team, and they would think the board was running the district. I knew it was not a good idea.

So, in front of the entire board, I immediately made my objection known. I said, "Guys, I understand that you might think this is a good idea, but please let me tell you why it's not." I then went through my list of concerns. Finally, I mentioned that my contract had a clause that stated I would be included in all closed sessions, except when discussing my yearly evaluation. In the end, the board agreed, and the board members' plan to meet by themselves was never enacted. I still believe that if I had let them do that, it would have been the start of the board trying to micromanage me and essentially run the district.

Unfortunately, I have seen instances in which the board successfully inserted themselves into daily decision-making. In one instance, when a new superintendent was hired, this particular type of board member essentially tried to run the district. No decision could be made without his approval, and board members were inserted on interview committees and even began to evaluate staff members. The superintendent now had to deal with the consequences.

Since the superintendent had allowed and even supported these practices in his early tenure to get in good favor with the board, he was now faced with essentially having a co-superintendent who had no knowledge of school leadership, no degree in education, and no clue about how to run a school district. The superintendent had enabled this and helped set his own trap, and now he was caught in a micromanagement nightmare.

Sometimes we have to sleep in the beds we make. And once you set a precedent for letting board members become daily decision-makers, you are likely setting yourself up for a short tenure, ending with poor morale throughout the district, school leaders leaving in droves, and eventually a rotten culture that will take years to rebuild. When your key administrators know you are running every decision by the school board, and your main job seems to be keeping board members happy, it leads to an erosion of trust between you and your leadership team.

POLITICAL ACTIVIST

As I write this book, we are seeing a new type of school board candidate—the political activist. School board members, by definition, should be nonpolitical and nonpartisan. School board candidates, at least in Texas, do not run in political primaries, and their party affiliation is not on the ballot.

However, we have recently seen school board candidates take on hot-button social issues hyped on television and social media, and running school board campaigns based on divisive racial issues. These candidates announce themselves as "Christian Conservative Republicans" in ad campaigns and denounce their opponents as trying to indoctrinate our kids with communist and socialist views. After being elected, some of these people go as far as sponsoring nationally known political activists to come into communities and tout the ideas of indoctrination, telling parents they should pull their kids out of the same local schools where they serve on the boards!

Most members who fall under this category see the school board as their launchpad to other political aspirations. Being on a school board gives them a monthly opportunity to pontificate on a variety of issues, stir up their base of supporters, and show that they are tough on whatever issue is the topic of the day, month, or year. Needless to say, those who are elected with these goals in mind are not your best board members and can turn a supportive and helpful body into one that is divisive and toxic.

ROLE OF A BOARD MEMBER

Commonsense leaders know there is a distinct line between the role of a board member and that of a superintendent. They each serve an important role, but they are very different. The role of a board member is to discuss and vote on policies that affect the district. The role of the superintendent is to manage the daily operations of the district. When these roles overlap, you have the beginnings of some major problems.

The role of a board member should be simple. If you draw a line on a piece of paper and write "policy" on one side and "daily operations" on the other side, that is really all you need to know. Board members should stay on their side of the paper—the policy side.

The school board, working with the superintendent, should set the goals and vision for the district. They represent the community and should have a good pulse on what the community wants and expects from their schools. They should also set and adopt policies that guide how the district operates, based on the laws of the state and federal governments.

One of the most important things the school board does is hire and evaluate the superintendent. This is the only employee a school board should interview and hire, and they should take this job extremely seriously. The board should assess the superintendent and ensure that they are working toward the goals the board has set for the district.

The other important role of the school board is to adopt a budget and set a tax rate. Obviously, school personnel, the superintendent, and the business office have a lot to do with developing a budget and making recommendations, but the school board has final authority to approve it or not.

Finally, the school board is a link to the community. They are elected officials, and their job is to make sure the community's interests are represented at school board meetings and during interactions with the superintendent.

ROLE OF THE SUPERINTENDENT

On the other side of the line is the "daily operations" role. This is the job of the superintendent and why the school board pays the superintendent to oversee operations of the district. To function efficiently, the superintendent has to act on matters daily without concern that the school board may not approve. Hiring and firing personnel, evaluating employees, and normal school operations are the responsibilities of the superintendent.

Unfortunately, in many schools, these lines get blurred. School board members get involved in areas in which they have no experience or expertise, and they attempt to wield authority where, as board members, they should not have authority. This blurring of the lines causes some districts to begin a downward spiral that can be a real mess for the next school board and superintendent to clean up.

SCHOOL BOARD MEETINGS

One oft-overlooked area in school leadership preparation programs is how to operate a school board meeting. In a time when board meetings and board members are becoming more political—and constituents are using board meetings to advance their political views—it is important for school leaders to understand some key concepts to help the school board run a good meeting.

One key fact I must state is that a school board meeting is just that—the board's meeting. This is when, usually once a month, board members come together to do the business of the district. As long as the board officers are operating within the law, you can make suggestions for making the meetings run smoothly, but at the end of the day, it is the board members' meeting. It is not the superintendent's meeting. I have found that certain elements help board meetings go smoothly—while other factors can make them a once-a-month fiasco.

I used to encourage my school board to operate their meetings in the following way:

- Start with a welcome, and always have some type of student recognition (more on this later).

- Have a "consent agenda" that groups common discussion points into a single agenda item so that the board can approve the grouped items in one action. And be sure to move quickly through the mundane board requirements, such as approving minutes.

- Have a director present a report about their department.

- Get into the main action items of the meeting.

- Include an executive session if needed.

- Finish the meeting by addressing a brief item related to personnel—hiring, firing, and resignations, for example.

That is an ideal setup for most board meetings. Now, let's discuss these items further, along with some of the nuances of a well-run meeting and how to avoid common pitfalls.

Length of Time

Nobody wants to sit through a six- to eight-hour board meeting—nobody!—especially after having put in a full day of work before the meeting even starts. My goal as superintendent was to help my board execute an efficient meeting and take care of district business but not waste any time. Over the course of my tenure, my school board meetings generally lasted two hours tops, with the vast majority being closer to an hour. By structuring the meeting properly and having some agreed-upon rules, a monthly meeting does not have to be a monthly beating.

Student Recognition

After the initial welcome and formalities, our meeting started with positive student recognition. Kicking off a board meeting by reminding everyone why we were there—students—set the tone for a positive meeting. This didn't need to take a lot of time, but each month, we recognized individual students or groups of students who had done things to shine a positive light on our school district.

By having their principal or coach introduce them to the board with some nice things to say, our meetings started with smiling faces, happy parents, and a reminder to board members and audience members of our preferred focus. Each student received a special pin to remind them of the recognition, and the parents got a minute to take photos of their children with me or the board to share with friends and family. This was always a great way to start a meeting.

Public Comments

After student recognition, we inserted public comments into our agenda. This was a time for citizens to sign up to speak to the board on any topic. Depending on the school district, the board can impose certain rules and limitations on citizens, but in most cases, a parent or other concerned community member can stand in front of the school board and say anything they want.

Most board policies have limits on how long a person can speak—usually three to five minutes—and most policies say this time cannot be used to talk about specific employees or board members. Policing this can be challenging, and the board president and officers must be willing to jump in and cut off a person who breaks these simple rules. Unfortunately, not all board officers have the ability or desire to assert this, so sometimes public comments can turn ugly. This is also an important time to reiterate that this is the board's meeting, so it is not your job as superintendent to jump in and enforce their policies.

One good thing about the portion of the meeting that allows public commentary is that the board and administration are not supposed to comment, respond to questions, or otherwise engage the speaker. So, if you can endure a few minutes of listening to complaints or accusations, you can move on with your meeting. My opinion is that these parents and citizens should handle the majority of these complaints by addressing the issues privately with appropriate school personnel. Unfortunately, in this time of hate and vitriol, some citizens just want to make a public scene, hoping it will go viral so they can impress their social media followers. I have heard very few public complaints at a board meeting that accomplished anything other than riling up a subsection of a community or giving the speaker some political clout.

Consent Agenda

After public comments, it is time to get on with the meat of the meeting. I liked to lump as much as possible into a section called a "consent agenda." The consent agenda allows a governing body to combine and approve a lot of regular, mundane, and noncontroversial agenda items into one. By doing this, it allows the board to have a motion, a second, and a vote on all of these items at once, rather than going through that process for each one.

Typical items on a consent agenda include approving the minutes, expenditures for the month, yearly vendor contracts, and other noncontroversial items that need little to no discussion. The good thing about placing as many items as you can on the consent agenda is that if a board member wants to discuss something on the consent agenda, they can ask that this one item be pulled off and voted on separately. Smart use of the consent agenda is a great way to condense time in a board meeting.

Department Reports

After the consent agenda, I liked to feature one department each month. I used this for board and community education, and to let board members know more about how the school operated. This also allowed me to put my directors in front of the public to highlight their areas of specialty. I told my directors to be fairly brief, but I wanted the board and the public to know about the departments' employees, their goals for the year, and some fun facts that might raise a few eyebrows. After the directors' presentations, board members usually had some good follow-up questions, and the board left with a new appreciation for a department they may have initially known little about.

When the foodservice director reports on how many thousands of meals are served each day, or the transportation director announces how many miles the buses traveled last year, it often amazes the board and members of the public who may have taken these departments for granted. When the athletic director reports on how many teams we are fielding and what percentage of our student body is involved in athletics, it helps explain why a considerable amount of money is spent on supplies, coaching stipends, and travel.

One department report each month gets all departments in front of the board at least once a year, takes up very little time in the meeting, and gives your administrators some much-deserved recognition.

Action Items

After the department report, go into action items. These are items on the agenda that need to be presented to the board, cleared of any questions, and then voted on individually by board members. If the action item is voted on affirmatively, the new policy goes into effect or purchases can be made, depending on the item.

When it comes to action items, it is imperative that you, as a leader, prepare your board for what is coming. Sometimes, on particularly detailed or controversial issues, you should bring it up at a monthly meeting as information only, and then bring it back the following month as an action item. Give the board some background information, answer the questions you know they will have, and at the end of your presentation, make a recommendation. Don't leave it up to the board to decide what to do without any information to back up the recommendation. It is your job as the educational leader to do the homework, the research, and all other work necessary before bringing an action item to the board. When you do, it should come in the form of a recommendation. When the board votes, they certainly don't have to vote the way you want them to, but at least you have made your recommendation known.

Executive Sessions

An executive session is a closed portion of a board meeting where a governing body can adjourn in private to discuss confidential matters. It is important to know there is a specific list of things a board can discuss in an executive session. These include discussions about the purchase or lease of property, personnel issues, the superintendent's evaluation or contract, and issues that require consultation with the school's attorney. The board is not supposed to go into executive sessions to talk about anything other than these specific issues. And they should never vote or even canvass votes in executive sessions about an item that must be voted on in public.

If the board is discussing the purchase of a piece of property for a new school, they can discuss the specifics, price, and needs in closed session, but they should not vote on the real estate purchase until they are back in open session acting on an agenda item. As easy as this is to write, it is much harder to handle in real life. Most board members don't like speaking publicly at board meetings, but you get them in a closed session and get ready! They talk about their children's teachers, how we need to fire a coach, and the height of the grass at the school's entrance. These items are not on the agenda and technically should not be discussed in closed sessions, but it is hard to police, and an item related to personnel can encompass a lot of gray area.

It helps when you have a strong board officer who has been through a training program on board meetings and will inform the board if they are straying off topic or discussing an issue that should not be discussed in closed session. I have known several board officers who were very good at this, and it really should be up to the board to police themselves. If they ask your advice, certainly offer it, or if you see that executive sessions are being used for the wrong reasons, perhaps sit down privately with your board officers to share your observations. However, at the end of the day, it is their meeting.

Also note that executive sessions should be confidential. Some extremely sensitive issues are discussed behind closed doors, and some information could cause serious problems if it were to get out to the public. I have had to inform my board about potential arrests of employees for drug use, alcohol use, and even sexual encounters with students. These are not good conversations, but it is important to let the board know about a situation before it makes front-page news.

I once had to inform my school board that a high-profile member of our community was likely getting arrested for an affair with a high school student. The investigation was ongoing, but I knew that once the information got out, it would be shocking to our entire community. I implored them to maintain confidentiality, and I did not disclose the name of the person under investigation because it may have been too juicy for even the most zip-lipped board member to resist telling someone. In the end, the arrest was made without the information leaking beforehand. The board members and I established a great amount of respect for one another due to this incident. They knew I would never hide information from them since they proved they could be trusted even under top-secret conditions.

I was very lucky in my career to work predominantly with board members who understood the sensitive nature of these meetings and the confidentiality they required. I normally had no worries telling my board anything, knowing it was unlikely to leave the room. When I went into a new school, I always had a detailed talk with my board about the importance of confidentiality in executive sessions. I told them I wanted to be able to be honest with them and give them as much information as I had. Further, as long as I knew this information was not going to leak, I would trust them. I also cautioned that if I heard things "on the street" that I had disclosed only in executive sessions, I would have to withhold the most sensitive information to avoid potential lawsuits or libel claims that could be filed against board members if sensitive information were leaked. I never had a bad incident related to leaked information from board members. However, I have seen colleagues have a terrible time controlling information leaks from their board.

One thing to note regarding executive sessions is that if they are held at the end of a meeting, they can be lengthy. I worked in one district where the board adjourned to executive session and stayed behind closed doors for several hours while the administrative staff sat twiddling their thumbs in the lounge. It was a colossal waste of time.

What works well is to schedule the executive session before the public meeting. By scheduling the executive session at 5:00 and the public meeting to begin at 6:00, you establish a time limit for that portion of the meeting. The board does not want to continue in closed sessions while fifty people are waiting for the public meeting to start, so they are usually good about staying on track and finishing their business within the allotted hour.

If you can't finish legitimate discussions in the one-hour slot, the board can go back to closed session after the agenda is completed. I remember rarely doing this, as you can almost always cover executive session items within one hour.

BOARD MEETING PREPARATION

I asked my board to be prepared before they came to each meeting, and my goal was to make the public meeting as much of a formality as I could. I did a few things to help with this. The most important was the use of what I called "board notes."

I attached my board notes to the packet of information I sent to the board several days before the meeting. In these board notes, I went through the entire agenda and, in layman's terms, briefly described each agenda item, noted the facts surrounding it, and made my recommendation. A board member could read my board notes and be prepared for the meeting. I always attached a lot of background information as well, but members relied most on the board notes. At the end of my notes, I also implored the board to call me with any questions or concerns so I could hopefully answer any pertinent questions before the meeting. If board members protested or questioned an issue or proposal during the meeting, especially if they wanted statistics or data we didn't have at our fingertips, I politely stated that if the board member had just called or emailed prior to the meeting, I would have had the information ready.

Unfortunately, on some items, mainly those involving politically charged issues, some board members like to use public meetings to pontificate and let constituents know where they stand. I noticed this mostly when discussing items such as school safety, resource and police officers, and the potential of arming staff members. As these are deeply divisive topics, depending on your community, sometimes board meetings become a vehicle for discussions about social politics.

BOARD EMAILS

One technique to get information to the board during weeks between meetings is the use of a confidential email to board members. In one of our first meetings, I explained how this type of communication must work.

It is illegal for board members to meet in a quorum and discuss school business outside of a board meeting that is properly announced. So, if issues came up that were highly volatile or controversial—and newsworthy—I felt I had to get this information to the board before they saw it elsewhere. Rather than calling special meetings, I emailed. These emails always had a subject line that looked like this: *****Confidential Board Information, Read ONLY*****

This alerted members to very important information that did not warrant a reply, especially not a "reply all," which could constitute an unlawful deliberation among board members. I excluded employees' names in case the emails were to leak, but I might inform the board, for instance, that a student or staff member was being arrested.

My board always appreciated the confidential emails. It kept them in the loop, avoided surprises on the evening newscast, and let them know I was being open and honest with them even about sensitive topics.

I also used these emails to inform the board of any particularly inflammatory decision I was about to make. While not really a board issue, if I was planning to fire a principal mid-year for misconduct or insubordination, or close school for a weather event, I wanted them to know about it. I told them in my email that if they wanted to discuss this further, to call me by a specified time or I was going to move forward with my decision. On the rare occasion that a board member called, I was able to give them more specific information and almost always got their support for whatever decision I was making.

BOARD COMMITTEES

Sometimes it is necessary to establish board committees to work on specific items, new policies, bond issues, superintendent search committees, and other special projects. But these committees, if left unchecked, can become monsters! When I was preparing for an interview to become the superintendent in a highly desirable location in Texas, I noticed that all of the board meetings lasted until well after midnight. I also noticed that on the agenda each month, a board member gave a report on an assigned department.

Each board member was placed "in charge" of a department—curriculum, finance, athletics, foodservice, maintenance, and so on—and would lead meetings with "their departments" throughout the month. Then at each month's board meeting, they reported, in excruciating detail, about their department. Since I thought this was a clear violation of the appropriate division of roles and responsibilities between board members and superintendents—policy versus everyday operations, remember?—I approached the topic in my interview.

The interview started off well, but as is characteristic, I asked as many questions as they did. When I broached the topic of why board meetings lasted so long and why board members appeared to be in charge of departments, the tone of the interview changed. The board members who liked being in charge of the departments had no intention of changing their process. They felt it was working fine, so I would have to accept it if I took the job.

This was a great job in a great location, and I told the board I would be proud to lead their school. Further, I would do a great job, and they would be proud they hired me. "But," I said, "I just can't accept a job where the board is in charge of our departments." I went through all my reasons, talking about staff morale, who was really running the district, and the enormous amount of time they were wasting, in my opinion. At this point, I knew I wasn't getting the position and would not have accepted it under those circumstances.

As I exited my interview, a board member ran after me in the parking lot. He said, "Dr. Largent, I just want to thank you for what you said in there. Three of us wanted to hire you on the spot, but the other four were not about to give up their control." I appreciated that he took the time to tell me that, and I could tell this was a dysfunctional and difficult board. I remembered what Dr. Bob Thompson told us in his Superintendent's Academy: "It's their kids, their schools, and their money. If you don't feel like you are a good fit, don't take the job."

Chapter Nine

SHOW ME THE MONEY— AND MANAGE IT, TOO

OF ALL THE DEPARTMENTS IN THE SCHOOL, THE BUSINESS office, which embodies school finance, is the one that can most quickly end your tenure. As superintendent, you are the ultimate steward of millions of dollars of taxpayer money. If you mismanage money, use it for noneducational purposes, or do something illegal, you can and probably should be fired immediately. A well-run business office can make your job go smoothly, make the school board look like heroes, and become an integral part of making a model for other districts to follow.

I am not a CPA, so crunching numbers, calculating revenue streams, and figuring out how to maximize tax rates are not my forte. Some superintendents love that part of the job, but not me. Because of that, it was always imperative that I had someone I could trust and who was knowledgeable (in that order) as my CFO or assistant superintendent for finance. When dealing with millions of dollars, you'd better have someone in that CFO chair you are confident in and know that person shares your values and goals.

TRUST IS A MUST

I was fortunate to have worked with two of the most knowledgeable and ethical people in the school business. Lesa Jones in Rusk ISD and Dobie Williams in Granbury ISD were both top-notch professionals in their work ethics, and I never questioned their motives or decision-making processes. They were both well-liked by staff, and school board members trusted the information they brought each month and during budget time. Because of the trusting partnership we developed, anytime money was needed for a project, they found it in the budget to make it work. They trusted that if I came to them with a project, it was necessary, so they committed to finding a way to fund it.

Unfortunately, I also worked with a CFO who could not be trusted, felt that they had the final say on purchases, and had the entire department set up so no decision could be made without their approval. This caused horrible morale issues that permeated the whole district due to the backlog of requests, poor decision-making, and general lack of trust among staff.

As I did anytime I came to a new district, I tried to lay out my expectations and get all the existing people on board with my new way of thinking. Unfortunately, despite my best efforts, this person and I never got on the same page. Due to a huge lack of trust, I had to bring on a new person. After I did so, the changes in the department were drastic, and morale improved immediately. Having the right people in key positions is absolutely critical, especially in an area like school finance.

FUNDAMENTALS OF SCHOOL FINANCE

Since I am admittedly not a finance guy, I always tried to make school finance as simple as possible. My simplified synopsis of how school finance works, at least in Texas, is this:

Revenue

In Texas, the school gets the majority of its revenue from local property taxes, with some additional state and federal dollars. To collect local property taxes, the taxing authority uses property values multiplied by the current tax rate. If you own a $200,000 home, and the tax rate is $1 per $100 of valuation, you would pay $2,000 in taxes for that particular year. Any change in either the property value or the tax rate will result in a different calculation in subsequent years.

Even though this lets you know how the property tax system generates dollars, there is a key calculation in Texas that tells a district how much of these dollars they can keep. Through the "Robin Hood" plan, a district with particularly high property wealth keeps only a portion of the dollars generated locally and sends the balance to the state to be distributed to other, less property-wealthy districts. This has been a point of much consternation for decades, but nevertheless, it is the current law.

The dollars a district is allowed to keep are generated on a weighted average daily attendance (WADA) calculation. The quick explanation for WADA is that each student has a formula attached to them. A regular student equals one ADA. If a student is in special education, career and technical classes, speech therapy, or a multitude of other special services, they are given an additional "weight." So, a special education student who requires all-day supervision from a trained nurse may be given a weight of 3.0 or more.

If a district has 5,000 students in average daily attendance, after attaching the formulas and doing the calculation, the WADA will be much higher than the actual number of students in attendance. The state then comes up with a number that is the value for each WADA. Simply by multiplying your WADA by the value of each ADA, you get the amount of money your school will be able to keep and put in the budget. Much has been made about how difficult school finance is, and how no one can understand it, but what I described above is really how it works. It's not rocket science, but it takes some understanding in order to not be overwhelmed.

Other revenue sources are usually targeted, such as federal dollars for foodservice, specific dollars for at-risk students, grants a school may be eligible for, and so on. Other sources are from ticket sales, advertising, marketing, and other methods of generating local revenue. By combining all of these sources into a budget, you may project the total revenue you can expect to generate and spend in the coming year.

Expenditures

Now that you have money to spend, how do you set up an expenditure budget to disperse all that money? As you might imagine, we do that by setting up an intricate system of numbers that methodically places every dollar in the budget into a specific place—usually in broad categories such as personnel and supplies, then broken down further into subsets of numbers. By the time a school budget is built, just by looking at the budget codes, one can tell which department the dollars are allocated to, what campus or grade level it goes to, and what it is used to pay for. This can seem complicated for an outsider, but when you see the function and object codes and how each dollar is allocated in a line-item budget, it is easy to understand.

After you have your revenues calculated and your wish-list expenditures in the budget, it is simply a matter of looking at the bottom line. Do you have enough revenue to cover your projected expenditures? If so, you can proceed with taking your budget to the school board for final approval. If not, you need to look at ways to make the budget work.

COMMONSENSE TIP FOR FINANCE

Be conservative with your numbers. If a school district is growing, it is sometimes necessary to project growth in your calculations. By calculating larger student numbers than you currently have, you increase the amount of money you will be able to keep in your budget. Just know that if you miss your calculation and student numbers do not grow at the rate you projected, the state will ask for that money back. I have seen this maneuver cost superintendents their jobs. They build a budget based on growth projections, spend all the money in the budget, then realize the student numbers did not grow as much as projected. Having to write multiple million-dollar checks to the state for your miscalculation does not lead to good school board relations.

THE SUMMER PROJECT METHOD

I recommend all superintendents use my summer project method to take care of big-ticket items and yearly maintenance issues. Keeping up with regular replacement cycles for HVAC, lighting, roof replacement, buses, floor replacement, painting, and such keeps these issues from piling up.

In a normal budget year, with student numbers growing slightly, and using conservative numbers in a budget, you can almost always expect that you will not spend all the money in the budget. In larger schools, the dollars left in each line item, even though they may be few, can add up and leave you with quite a large surplus of funds. These leftover funds do not carry over to the next year's budget but are put in a fund balance, the school's equivalent to a savings account.

My summer project exercise normally started in December, with principals and department directors submitting wish lists of things they wanted to be done in the upcoming summer. Working with my maintenance and transportation directors, we developed replacement cycles for roofs, HVAC systems, and buses. Each year, we knew which campus would need a new roof, how many twenty-year-old HVAC systems we needed to replace, and how many buses to add to the fleet. My principals submitted requests for hallways and classrooms to be painted, tile floors that needed replacing, and other renovations or additions they wanted us to consider.

By early spring, we had a list of all the potential summer projects, then spent time with our administrative team going through each request, the projected cost, and whether or not we felt it was necessary or feasible. By working through this list, we came up with a final list of projects we would recommend to the school board. After receiving their approval to move forward with our selected projects, we sent requests out for bids on all the projects with contractors understanding we wanted them to start the day school was out and be finished in plenty of time to avoid a disruption to the start of our next school year.

As we neared the end of a school budget year in mid-spring, my CFO could accurately project how much money would be left in the budget to pay for the requests. If we needed to complete particularly large-ticket items, we made it clear to the school board that we may be tapping into the fund balance to pay for those items. Over the years, it was amazing the number of projects and maintenance issues we were able to accomplish without adversely affecting our finances. Too often, these types of projects and upkeep issues are left undone, making facilities age quickly and appear dated, and robbing taxpayers of the lifespan they should expect of public facilities. I urge you to add this method of summer projects to your yearly to-do list.

WHAT I LEARNED FROM PAUL ZEEK: ORGANIZE!

Paul Zeek was the head athletic trainer at Lamar University. I began communicating with him while I was in high school, and upon graduation, he offered me a scholarship to become an athletic trainer at LU for four years. Working under his leadership, I learned the basics of how to run an organization.

Mr. Zeek (I never could call him Paul) set high expectations for our training department, was highly respected in the athletic training circles, and was one reason I chose to attend college close to home. Through his leadership, I learned how to write work schedules, create simple budgets and bid sheets, and create checklists of supplies, equipment, and tasks to ensure we were prepared for anything. His influence on me, his work ethic, and his attention to detail certainly carried over for the remainder of my career.

FUN FACTS ABOUT TAXES

Nobody likes to pay taxes, but I do like it when the police show up if someone breaks into my home, and I like it when the fire truck arrives if my house is on fire. I also like to drive on paved streets, have safe drinking water, and know that people follow some basic guidelines in my community.

The reality is, in a democratic, capitalistic society, we all pay taxes one way or another, and these dollars go to the federal, state, and local governments to allow them to operate financially. Public school is no different. Different states may collect taxes differently, and how the money is dispersed can vary, but financial support for public schools generally comes from taxes. In Texas, property taxes make up the bulk of our budgets, with some dollars flowing from the federal government as well.

As a leader, it is important to know the tax structure for the state in which you work. In Texas, we have a maintenance and operations (M&O) tax, and an interest and sinking (I&S) tax. These numbers added together make up the total school tax. Leaders should know about some clear distinctions between these two taxes:

M&O tax: Think of the M&O tax as the district's checkbook. It is used to pay the monthly utility and fuel bills, buy supplies, pay staff, and all the other things that go into running a school district. The M&O tax is always the higher number of the total tax rate. The M&O tax is a one-year revenue. Money from this tax is used to build a one-year budget. At the end of the fiscal year, any money left in the current budget goes into a fund balance, the equivalent of a district's savings account. The dollars in a fund balance can be carried over and saved from year to year, but the M&O budget must be built each year and cleared at the end of the year.

I&S tax: Think of the I&S tax as a special account used to pay the mortgage of a house. In a school's case, this is used to pay the note for bond issues. Any money received from the I&S tax can be used only to pay for debt service. It cannot be commingled with the M&O revenue and must remain separate.

A few people have confronted me regarding taxes, and they usually fall into two groups. One is the "I pay taxes, so…" group, and the other is the "Why do my taxes go up every year?" group. Let's look at both:

I pay taxes, so…

On several occasions, people in my community have come to me and said, "I pay taxes, so my child can do this or that." They seem to think that since they pay into the coffers to help run the district, this somehow gives them the authority to make decisions about how the school is run. I've seen parents refuse to pay to get into a ballgame to watch their kids play. "I pay taxes, so..."

Now, for a while, I tried to slow the parent down, talk them through the situation, and tell them I would try to help. After it was clear that tactic did not work, I did this. When someone mentioned they were going to do something inappropriate because they paid taxes, I said, "You know, I pay taxes to the county, too, but I don't borrow the county dump truck on the weekends or borrow a fire truck if I want to take the neighborhood kids for a ride." Usually, this has them scratching their head a little bit, trying to come up with a valid comeback.

Why do my taxes go up every year?

The other group includes constituents who believe taxes are too high, that we should never raise taxes, and that we should in fact lower taxes because they are such a burden. They normally complain about their home value increase, which raises the amount of taxes they have to pay.

Property taxes are based on the value of a property. In Texas, taxes are levied at one cent per hundred dollars of the property value. So, if you own a $100,000 home and the tax rate is one dollar, you pay $1,000 in taxes. Assuming the tax rate stays the same but the value of your home increases, you pay more taxes. If, the following year, your house increases to $125,000 in value, your tax levy is $1,250 per year due to the increase in value, even at the same tax rate.

This is a common issue in a lot of communities, especially those with growing populations, desirable locations, or properties that are particularly enticing, like waterfront or golf course homes. A technique that has worked for me when dealing with these complaints is to very matter-of-factly say, "I tell you what—if I write you a check right now for what the chief tax appraiser says is the value of your home, would you take it?" I have not had a single taker. That tells me the valuation is fair and likely too low.

In either case, taxpayers don't like paying taxes, and that is understandable. But when you can walk them through the scenarios regarding values and how money is distributed, you can at least help them understand more about the system and how it works.

BOND ISSUES

Bond issues are an animal all to themselves. If you are not familiar with what a bond issue is, think of it as a way to ask your community if you can go out and get a mortgage on a new property. That is really all it is. The district needs to purchase land, build new campuses, add on to schools, or do major renovations, and the only way to fund these projects is to take out a mortgage and pay it off over time. The bond issue process is the mechanism for schools to do this. The bond referendum is placed on a ballot for the voters in the school district to vote on, and if the referendum is approved, local taxpayers agree to fund this new "mortgage" over time.

Depending on the community, the issues, the politics in the area, and the support for local schools, these bond issues can be a simple process that is overwhelmingly approved or an ugly campaign that takes on the optics of conspiracy theories, misinformation, and outright lies. But you can do some things to give your bond issue every chance of being successful, as I outline here.

Visible, Necessary, and with Full Community Support

These are the easiest bond issues to pass. When I took my first job as superintendent, our main high school building was an old Work Projects Administration (WPA) facility built in the 1930s. It held a lot of community sentiment, as I would learn during this process, but the need for a new high school building in our slowly growing community was obvious to almost everyone. After working with a committee of people and looking at options, our bond capacity (how much money we could raise in our current tax structure), and other intricacies of the project, we rolled out our bond referendum to the community.

In this small community, we didn't need to do a lot of campaigning. I made charts and handouts showing exactly what we wanted, and we held several community events at the school, where I conducted presentations for our proposal. We shared images of what our new facility would look like, statistics on how this would increase capacity to handle future growth, and facts about the minimal tax implications for local citizens.

Anyone who wanted information about the bond was able to ask me, personally. Community members were very clear that they did not want the old WPA building torn down. Almost everyone in the community had gone to school there, so they wanted to protect their history. We quickly revised our plan, letting our community know the old building would remain on-site and continue to be used in the district.

In the end, because we were so transparent and visible, and included our community's wants and needs, the bond election passed with 82 percent of the vote, a landslide almost unheard of in election terms.

Bond Planning

When I became superintendent at a much larger district in a suburban area, the landscape was decidedly different. This was known as predominantly a retirement community, with several massive gated golf course communities encompassing thousands of homes. When I took the job, several people told me I would never be able to pass a bond issue because the retirees had no connection to or interest in our schools. In fact, the last time a bond issue had been attempted, it failed miserably. This task would be daunting, but I took it as a challenge.

With recent failures in mind, I knew we had to be precise in every move. The needs of the district were glaring—decades-old facilities ill-equipped for present-day learning environments and community growth that demanded we add classroom space to accommodate future growth. The needs were apparent to those of us on the inside, but getting that message out to our community would be key.

My first task was to come up with a list of needs from our community. When I arrived at this new district, one of my first big decisions was to begin a process of comprehensive K–12 strategic planning. We began the process with a community-wide survey, which received thousands of responses, and followed that up with a strategic team of about one hundred members, including staff, students, parents, and community leaders. This large group was broken down into many different subgroups that met weekly for the better part of a semester to each focus on one area. Curriculum and delivery, finance, learning environments, community service, athletics, and extracurricular activities were just some of the breakout groups.

I was active in all of the groups, rotating to hear the discussions in each, offering my opinions and insight, and trying to gauge interest on key issues. The facility group became the one with the biggest plans and dollars attached, so I began spending a lot of time with this group to help formulate a plan. One of the first things we had to do was find an architect who could work with us to develop a plan and help us present to our community the transformation of our entire school district.

Pro Tip: when planning bond programs, include something in the bond that touches as many different campuses and areas as possible—academics, fine arts, safety issues, playgrounds, and so on. These are all areas that can make a huge difference in support for a bond. Think of what you are presenting to your public as "something for everyone," even though that may not necessarily be the case. If parents see all the money raised by the bond is being spent on one campus or one program such as athletics, many will be turned off and either be against the bond or simply not show up to vote.

In Granbury, our community made it very clear through our strategic planning process that they wanted to see a focus on career and technical education. When we presented a plan for our high school that included a 100,000-square-foot addition totally dedicated to career and technical programs, our community was excited. We also added to all of our campuses new safe and secure entries, which was an important topic at the time. Every campus in our district had a slight change in appearance by creating these new entries and lobby areas. Even though the cost was somewhat negligible in the total cost of the bond, parents and staff at those campuses had something they could get behind and support. I have seen even lower-cost items, like new equipment and shade systems on playgrounds, bring out support for bonds from parents of elementary school children.

Heed this word of warning: athletics and athletic facilities can be a controversial topic when presenting a bond issue to the public. I have seen relatively low-cost athletic upgrades sink bonds in some cases. I would caution that if you plan to make athletics a big part of your bond, do your homework and find creative ways to incorporate other programs and opportunities for students to use the proposed facilities.

Some community members feel too much money is already spent on athletics, even though typically only about 3 percent of a school's budget is spent in the sports arena. But the general public sometimes sees turf fields, huge press boxes with elevators and hospitality rooms, and giant jumbotrons for scoreboards as a waste of taxpayer dollars. Each community is different, and you have to accurately gauge the pulse in your district before moving forward with plans. By incorporating video production and media classes into the press box, however, as a way for students to produce work and prepare for a career in media, you can sometimes justify the expense to your community and gain support. But before I made athletics a major part of a bond program, I carefully weighed the pros and cons, and whether or not including this would be a net gain or net loss of votes.

A Political Campaign

As we began looking at architects and going through our selection process, I was much less interested in pictures of pretty buildings and prior construction projects, and much more intrigued with the tools the firm planned to use to help our district pass a bond issue. With the bond failures our district had experienced before my arrival, we could design all the pretty buildings we wanted, but unless we could pass the bond, they would never come to fruition.

The architectural firm we selected had the usual impressive list of clients, but they also had something other firms did not offer. They connected us with a partner whose sole focus was helping us market our bond. This was not going to be anything like the bond program I ran in the small school where we passed my first bond as a superintendent. This was going to be very different.

The marketing professionals were confident that if I were to follow their lead, we could pass this bond. As we formulated our campaign, we left no stone unturned. While still in the planning stages, we hired a political pollster in Austin, Texas, to survey our community and report back to us with results. After our polling, we had a clear path of what projects our voters would support, the amount of money in a bond they would support, and the maximum tax rate our voters would tolerate. We used this data as we finalized our bond plans.

Next was the formation of a political action committee (PAC). The PAC had no school leaders involved, met away from school facilities, and worked on their own agenda. Their focus was to get the word out in support of the bond, something we at the school could not do.

In bond election laws, the school's role has to be that of only providing factual information. It can't spend money or time promoting a "yes" vote and can only put together information so the public can make an informed decision. These lines are sometimes blurred because everyone knows that if the school is presenting a bond issue, its administrators are in favor of the bond, but this is a legal requirement, so follow the law.

We put together a really good presentation about what the bond would do, why we needed it, and what it would cost taxpayers. In our presentation, we included a lot of "before" photos of our current facilities followed by "after" images—concept drawings of the plans. Contrasting a 1970s-style home economics class-room with a picture of a commercial culinary kitchen showed everyone the stark differences in what we had and what the bond would provide to students. Showing a variety of current learning environments and then showing new spaces with modern, more functional seating and technology had an impact on those who saw our presentation. I made this presentation dozens of times to every group I could get in front of.

We also focused on our retirement communities by making presentations at their various social groups. We found that, despite what I had heard, the retirees were very interested in what we were doing, and many were former educators or had family members in education. They were supportive of our plans, and we felt we had their vote.

In many communities around this time period, schools that went out for bond issues were immediately met with the anti-tax crowd, who actively campaigned against any tax increase for any reason. Many times, campaigns were funded by outside groups, and this was when the Tea Party movement was getting a lot of attention around the country. By flooding a community with "Vote No New Taxes" signs and distributing propaganda through the local media outlets, these groups were often successful in defeating bond issues in communities.

When we began the speaking tour, one of my first stops was to the local Republican Club, which at the time was composed primarily of far-right activists who were against new taxes and most other signs of progress. Despite this, I asked to speak to the group and present our plan. We filled a room that night, with about half of the crowd being club members and the other half composed of supporters who just wanted to see fireworks!

As I began my presentation, I was crystal clear about many facts I knew they didn't know but would have questions about. We had the lowest tax rate of almost every district in the Dallas–Fort Worth area, and even if our bond passed, we would still have one of the lowest. I presented the pictures of what we had versus what we could have, and I made a plea that local schools are a main driver of the economy, real estate, and sales tax for local businesses. Because I was prepared, I answered most of their questions before they had a chance to ask them. They never mounted public opposition to our campaign, and that surprised most of our school leaders who were expecting a fight. I doubt many of them voted for the bond, but the fact that they never formed a "Vote No" campaign certainly helped our cause.

One other strategy we used was to petition state and local govern- ment entities to host polling sites at our schools. Bond elections have historically low voter turnout, so we needed to be sure parents of students who would benefit from these new learning environments would be motivated to vote. So, we set up election opportunities at a couple of our larger, more visible campuses and scheduled large school events during early voting. This was an easy way for people to come see their children perform and, while they were there, be reminded to vote.

As we moved into early voting, we had to come up with a game plan to make sure as many people who supported the bond would actually go to the polls and vote. We employed a lot of differ- ent tactics. About a month before early voting began, our PAC began calling all voters who had voted in the last three elections. The first call was to tell them a few specifics about the election, answer any questions, and gauge their interest in supporting the bond. Each person the PAC called was marked as a "supporter," a "no" vote, or a person who might be persuaded.

When early voting began, PAC members made a second call to remind supporters that voting had begun and we really needed their support at the polls. Obviously, our "no" voters did not receive a reminder call.

The next thing our PAC did was to request, through the Public Information Act, contact information for all parents and staff members. The PAC did not bombard these people with constant information, but over the course of a month or two, the list was used to send out information about the bond, what it contained, and why it was important for it to pass. As voting began, the list was used as a "get out the vote" tool, with reminder emails and letters to voters about when and where they could vote.

By using early voting information, as soon as voting began, we requested from our elections office a daily list of everyone who had voted. We had no idea which way they had voted, but we knew they had voted. By using this list and cross-checking it with our list of supporters and likely "no" votes, we had an idea of how we were doing in the early voting. As days went by, the PAC focused its calls only on supporters who had not shown up on the voter lists. The PAC's list of calls grew smaller, and we saw more supporters showing up on the voter lists. This tactic worked to perfection.

As the school is normally the largest, or one of the largest, employers in the area, it was critical that our staff voted. In order to win the election, we had to maximize our staff voting and assume the overwhelming majority would vote for the bond. We employed a few tactics to help with this. We got a little blowback from some of these tactics, so make your own judgment about what might work in your area. Nevertheless, this is what we did.

The first and easiest strategy was to constantly remind our staff, using my weekly email, of the upcoming election and the factual information related to the bond proposal. Next, as I did with every election, I implored staff to use their conference period, lunch break, or any other break in their day to go vote. I didn't want anyone to say they didn't have time or had no opportunity to vote, so I always gave staff an open invitation to leave campus and go vote. On several days during early voting, teams of retired teachers even came to our campuses to substitute for teachers so they could go vote. This was publicized, and the campus principals made a big deal of this, which encouraged even more staff to vote.

The next, slightly controversial, tactic was to use voting boards in teachers' lounges for staff to voluntarily sign on that they had voted. Each day, those who had voted the day before signed the board, and some wrote a comment, drew a smiley face, or just signed a "Go Vote" message next to their name. It was completely voluntary, but it gave staff a daily reminder that an election was going on and that they were vigorously encouraged to vote.

Some staff members felt this was over the line, a way to intimidate them into voting. I understood their sentiment to a degree, but I have always believed that when you take a paycheck from an organization, you owe them your loyalty if nothing else. It doesn't mean you should agree with or even vote for a bond, but it seemed the few people who had a problem with this tactic were the same lounge lizards who were never happy with anything going on in the school.

As for parents, we employed a different tactic. In addition to the PAC making contact and sending information, we used the district's phone system to send messages to all parents in our database. We were careful to only give factual information on these calls, but the message came from me or a campus principal, who recorded a message reminding parents that our bond election was going on now and to go vote.

On election night, I was at the local community center, the gathering place where election results were posted. When the early voting results were posted, our two bond propositions had received about 60 percent of the votes, so we were confident our bond proposal would be approved. When all the votes were tallied, Proposition 1, by far the most substantial of the two, had passed by 57 percent of the vote, and Proposition 2 had received over 60 percent—this in a community where the last bond proposals had failed.

I don't think just one factor caused our bond to be successful, but the strategies combined to give us the best chance. While I had a good handle on the strategic planning and putting together a good package to send to voters, the tactics we used to treat the election like a political campaign paid off.

Throughout the process, after the election was successful, we gave our community regular updates on the progress of our projects. Three years later, after all our construction was completed, it was amazing to go back and look at the concept drawings we presented to our community and compare them to the actual finished projects. It was like bringing an artist's rendering to life. In the end, our community was extremely excited about the transformation of our district and the opportunities it would give our students for decades.

SIMPLE TIPS FOR BOND PLANNING

- In the planning stage, involve as many stakeholders as you can manage, and ask for their input.

- Put together a package that gives *something* to everyone in the district.

- Have a realistic package that will be paid for with the least amount of tax burden on your community.

- Put together a comprehensive, factual presentation with before-and-after pictures, and present it to every group you can. Pay special attention to groups you believe will be against your proposal. Go to those groups, answer their questions, and let them decide.

- Run the bond election like a political campaign, applying tactics politicians use to get out their supporters.

- Do what you say you are going to do. Make your package completely transparent, and then deliver to your community what you said you would.

Chapter Ten

THE COGS IN THE GEARS OF A GREAT SCHOOL

"Leadership is about people; it's about inspiring people to believe that the impossible is possible."

—GIFFORD THOMAS

I FREQUENTLY TELL PEOPLE THE TIME I SPENT AT A VERY small school district as superintendent was probably the most valuable training. The reason is that, due to not having a director for every department at that small school, I had to learn about each department, how it was funded, related policies and laws specific to each, and some of the caveats that make each department unique. In the next few sections, I discuss several important departments in a school district.

HUMAN RESOURCES

The human resources department really works hand in hand with the finance department. Depending on the size of your district, it may be part of the business office or completely separate. I believe some common sense is necessary for a well-run HR department.

First, district employees need to know HR is there to help them. Interactions should be positive, and the best HR department heads constantly look for ways to add benefits, perks, and other services to show employees they are appreciated. New staff induction programs, year-long new teacher programs, and bringing in financial advisors, estate planners, and other experts to advise staff about how to position themselves for the future are all simple things the HR department can do to create a positive atmosphere. Incentives such as gift cards, monthly recognition programs, discount cards from area businesses, and gym memberships also let your employees know they are appreciated, and this is also a good way to get local businesses involved.

Helping with certification issues, paperwork, grievances, and negative evaluations are other ways HR personnel can be of assistance. My HR director at Granbury ISD, Wes Jones, was a perfect fit for his job. I joked with Wes that he could fire an employee for a violation of their contract and they'd hug him on the way out the door. He created such a great atmosphere in his department that employees knew he would do anything possible to help boost their employment. If an employee didn't work out, he went out of his way to make the separation genial.

One aspect I believe is important is the constant evaluation of health and insurance plans, third-party vendors, workers' comp, and every other program offered through HR. Some of the plans, like workers' comp, seem insignificant and low-cost. But upon further evaluation, you may find that more dollars are going through a particular program than you thought.

In one school where I was superintendent, we found that our workers' comp provider had a very small annual fee but was scalping us anytime there was a claim, making significant dollars in what I consider an underhanded way. Charges were masked as savings to the district when, in actuality, decisions about payouts for claims came from a state agency. For example, if a school receives a hospital bill for an employee's broken arm, the invoice may be for ten thousand dollars. After reviewing the bill, the state agency may only allow a charge of three thousand dollars. A portion of this seven thousand dollar "savings" is sometimes charged to the district in what I think is an unsavory way to make money. When my new CFO finally explained to me how the program was operating, I was clear on what was going on. By switching our business to Creative Risk Funding's product, *SchoolComp*, our district saved tens of thousands of dollars over the next few years.

Similar examples are found in almost every area of HR when contracts are involved. School leaders should frequently evaluate current providers as well as others in the market to get the best value and service to employees and the district. An annual checkup is necessary to maximize quality and value from these important services.

ATHLETICS

Athletics is the most visible department in any school district. It gets the most publicity and can significantly affect school culture. Schools with great athletic programs have a great amount of pride.

Unlike a classroom teacher, coaches put their performance on public display each time their team takes the field. As a former coach, I have great admiration for those who choose to dedicate their lives to coaching athletics and molding young student athletes. Time away from family, the mental and physical toll it takes on a person, and other challenging aspects of the job certainly make it a high-pressure but extremely rewarding profession.

I was fortunate in my career to work for several very successful coaches and be a part of winning traditions. I will always cherish the opportunity I had to watch and implement the work ethic and discipline it takes to be successful. My short time as a head baseball coach turning a perennial loser into a playoff team is still a highlight of my career.

If you ask any athletic director or head coach what their biggest obstacle is, almost unanimously they will say it is parents with unrealistic expectations. Athletics is one of the few departments in which some parents think they are experts. As a superintendent, I can count on one hand how many times a parent came to me to complain about the math or English curriculum, our method of calculating revenues and budget estimates, or the FDA regulations in our foodservice department. But if we happened to lose a game or our athletic program was not doing well, you could bet there were parents who claimed to know exactly why we were not winning. Their solutions almost always included firing coaches or making sure their child played more.

If you want to have a laugh, sit several rows behind a particularly engaged set of parents. A group of dads sitting together is the best group to observe. Over the course of a game, you can learn all kinds of things: "When we won the world championship in Buna that year when these kids were five years old, Johnny was an NFL prospect." Or "If the coaches would play Tucker at linebacker, he would stop them running up the middle on us like he did in the state championship game in Jacksboro when he was in fourth grade." Yep, if you can sit behind some dads at a ballgame, you will learn why your team is not winning. Heck, I've seen championship teams go deep into the playoffs, and parents were still unhappy because their son or daughter was not the star of the team.

When I was a principal and superintendent, I would ask to speak with the coaching staff at the beginning of each year. During those talks, I reiterated to them several factors:

Coaches are hired to help build a program. Aside from the parents, nobody cares if you go 10-0 in seventh grade because you had one kid who was better than everybody else and could run over, or past, everyone. Building a program means you develop players who love the game and will stay in the program until graduation. Over time, some kids who were great junior high players will move away, no longer improve, or lose interest in the sport. If you have invested all your time in letting one student be the star of the team, when they are no longer around, you have no one groomed to take their position.

This happened with my son. Justin was a small kid in junior high. He was not very tall and weighed about ninety-eight pounds in seventh grade. But he loved football. He could throw the ball and wanted to be a quarterback. Well, in his class, a few kids had matured a little quicker and were better football players at that age. Justin was at practice every day, but on game days, he rarely played. After doing that in seventh and eighth grade, he decided practicing in the Texas heat and the lack of playing time were no fun for him. So, he took up golf.

By the time he was a senior in high school, Justin was six foot four and weighed about 185 pounds, a prototype build for a quarterback. The 5A school we moved to tried to recruit him to play football his senior year, but by that time, he was dedicated to golf. He and his golf team went on to play in the 5A state golf championship, and he received a golf scholarship to play in college. Had those coaches in junior high kept him interested in football and let him play in games, his athletic career may have been totally different.

Hold a preseason meeting with parents. I expected my coaches to have a mandatory preseason meeting with parents. I also required that they establish a handbook for each sport that parents would review and then sign a statement indicating that they had received and understood it. This handbook was as elaborate as the coach wanted it to be, but I wanted guidelines for parents—practice schedules, expectations for riding the bus (or not) to and from games, how to handle playing-time issues, what to do if a student had to miss a game for family or other endeavors, and other pertinent issues. Having this mandatory meeting, going over all of these points in person, and then having the parent sign off took care of most potential problems.

How did we get parents to attend the meeting? One of the requirements was that before students could practice with the team, parents had to have a meeting with the coach. If they couldn't make the large group meeting, they could set up an individual meeting with the coach. Given these parameters, the majority of parents made it to the large group meetings. Athletes who did not want to miss practice made sure their parents were in attendance!

Be honest with players and parents. When I was a head coach, after the first few weeks of practice and before we began our season,

I used one day of practice to sit down with players individually while my assistants ran practice.

In these meetings, I told each player my honest evaluation of their talent level, where they needed to improve, and how I planned to use them on the team that year, and then I gave them a chance to ask questions. I told some players I didn't see them getting to play much, if any, that year. I told others they would likely be moving to junior varsity.

I always had a few kids on my team who wanted to be baseball players but were much better at running track. They were great runners but not great baseball players. I would tell them I thought they should focus on track, where they could help our program succeed. But I wanted them on the team, and their role might be to run bases as needed and be good teammates. As long as they were good with this, so was I. We won several games over the years due to pinch-running for a slower player late in a game with a track athlete, who could score from first base on a gapper in the outfield.

At these one-on-one meetings, I told my players their parents could come to me if they had questions or concerns. I was happy to sit down with parents about their child's evaluation. Only a few parents took me up on this over the years, and it never ended badly. Anytime I could talk face-to-face and openly, it almost always ended well.

At the end of each season, I went one step further with my honesty. I gave each player on my team their stats for the year. I meticulously kept stats on all my players throughout the year—pitching, hitting, fielding, and so on. Along with an evaluation on how to improve and specific skills to hone, I included a personalized workout for the off-season. I got more positive feedback from parents on this than on almost anything else I did. It was great for parents to see the actual statistics for their child, and they appreciated that I took the time to do it. If the athlete decided not to take my advice for off-season work, when they returned the following year, I had something to refer back to.

Athletics was an important part of my career, and I enjoyed it immensely. If coaches and athletic directors take these simple tips and adjust them to suit their needs, they can head off most problems before they start—and cause the superintendent fewer headaches and less time dealing with disgruntled parents.

TRANSPORTATION

Riding a bus seems to be a simple operation that shouldn't have a lot of issues. But coordinating rides to school for students ages three to twenty-four has its plethora of potential problems— finding drivers, front door pickup versus bus stop pickup, older kids with younger kids, multiple routes per day, being on time for pickups and drop-offs, how long to wait for students who are not at their stop, what happens if a parent gets on the bus to confront a driver, bus wrecks and breakdowns, and lost students, to name a few. Yes, plenty of transportation problems occur daily. Here are some commonsense ways to avert problems:

Directors. As with most jobs in school administration, having the right person is critical. Some people love the transportation business. They love seeing those big yellow buses leave before daylight each day and greeting them as they wrap up their evening routes as dark settles in. These people have a knack for attracting bus drivers and keeping them happy in their jobs. The most important attribute of a great transportation director is pride in independently taking care of any transportation-related problem and not letting it get to the central office. I worked with two directors, Thomas Parsons and Terry Slemmons, who took great care of their departments. Having the right director can save you hours of time dealing with parents who are upset about something related to their child's bus ride. And creating a team atmosphere, where drivers know they are appreciated, makes for the most successful transportation departments.

Drivers. Bus drivers are the first school employees many students see every day. Their demeanor can affect the start of the school day for some students. If the first thing a still-sleepy and groggy-eyed elementary school kid hears from a driver is a berating for being one minute late to their stop, it can start their day off on a bad note. Likewise, if they are met with a smile and treated with respect, positive relationships can form that last for years.

Hiring drivers is becoming more difficult today. Bus drivers work for little pay, keep odd hours (a couple of hours early and a couple of hours late), and are in a potentially volatile environment. Try driving a seventy-two passenger vehicle with your back to dozens of school-age kids. No potential problems there, huh? It takes a special kind of person to drive a school bus, and as I mentioned earlier, in order to hire and keep good drivers, directors must do as much as possible to let them know they are appreciated.

Many drivers, it seems, are retired from another line of work, and the quasi-part-time basis of driving a bus fits them perfectly. Others are parents of school-age children and want a job with the same hours and days that their kids are in school. Making a little extra money on the side and the benefit of insurance make it attractive for some people. Once on the job and having passed the certification tests, drivers must prove that they have the demeanor to deal with such a wide array of students. Finally, ideal drivers are dependable, know how important their job is, and commit to doing it long term.

Discipline. As mentioned earlier, when driving a bus with seventy-two children behind your back, incidents are going to happen, such as fighting or vandalism. Most buses are equipped with cameras these days, so the staff doesn't find out what actually happened until after the fact. But how a driver handles problems en route is critical. Years ago, and especially in rural areas, it was not uncommon for a driver to stop the bus, put the unruly child off the bus on the side of the road, and drive away. Obviously, that can't happen today, and with improvements in communication, the bus is always just a phone call or radio call away from assistance.

Discipline on a bus should be taken very seriously. I always took a hard line on bus discipline. We set up a program whereby unruly students lost the privilege of riding the bus. We normally gave them a three-day, one-month, and one-semester punishment, in that order. We reiterated to parents that riding a bus is a privilege and that we would not offer rides to kids who wouldn't behave on our buses. We worked with parents to assign seats or otherwise help students stay away from peers, but in the end, if they couldn't behave, they couldn't ride our bus. Knowing they would have to drive their kids to and from school was usually a strong incentive for parents to help us with this issue.

Technology. A lot of helpful tools, such as GPS and routing software, are now available for transportation departments. GPS monitoring allows the department and even parents the ability to know exactly where their bus is located, how fast it is moving, and the ETA at each stop. Routing software enables schools to know specific data on neighborhoods, the numbers of students in each household, and potential bus stops that allow for multiple pickups with minimal stops. And the instant communication with cell phones and two-way radios makes it easy to talk to drivers about potential problems or help with discipline, accidents, or breakdowns.

The transportation department sometimes goes overlooked in a school. By paying attention to hiring great people and providing them with the tools they need to be successful, this department can create a positive identity of goodwill for your school.

FOODSERVICE

Foodservice is another area, like transportation, that sometimes gets overlooked. For people outside of the school business, foodservice has negative connotations—long lines of kids waiting for the hair-netted lunch lady to serve food on industrial plastic trays. Well, times have changed, and there is a lot more to foodservice today.

For one, the regulations surrounding school lunches are long and cumbersome. Each meal must have the correct ratio of calories, nutritional content, portion size, and relative proportions of foods on the tray. Further, each particular part of the meal must maintain a specific temperature for food safety purposes. It takes a well-organized group of people to ensure daily lunches meet all the requirements.

Another issue around foodservice is the quality of the food and how it tastes. Finding foods that meet the nutritional requirements and still taste good make the job even more difficult. Some simple strategies when working with foodservice can help make this a popular part of your school district and not one that is ridiculed:

Taste. If you want to know what the kids like to eat, just ask them! I always urged my foodservice directors to periodically do surveys and taste tests with students to find out what they like. By having food samples and asking kids' opinions, you get honest responses about what tastes good and what doesn't. The other way to tell if kids don't like the food is the trash can test. If the entree of the day ends up mostly in the trash can, find another menu item to replace it. I have found that casseroles—anything with ground meat and English peas—and other meals that just don't look appetizing usually end up in the trash. For foodservice to be successful, find foods and menu items the kids enjoy.

Variety. It's very popular with students to set up a variety of kiosks throughout the cafeteria. Having several options spread out in the room—rather than forcing students to get in a long industrial line—gives students choices, allows staff to serve more efficiently, and generally makes lunch more enjoyable. We've tried kiosks for salad bars, some type of Tex-Mex offering, and a more traditional burger and chicken station that all met nutritional requirements. In some cafeterias, the staff got creative and decorated each kiosk to look like an authentic restaurant with graphics, funny sayings, or servers dressed to make it feel like a restaurant. In one school, we even built a coffee bar that sold Starbucks-type coffee with all different flavorings. It was a popular place for students and staff. Guests were amazed we had something like that in our high school.

With the right mix of foodservice leadership, a staff who loves their job, and regular student input, the foodservice department can become a very popular place where kids enjoy the food and the environment—not the industrial look and feel of old.

TECHNOLOGY

Of all the departments in a school, technology can be its own unique beast. Our schools cannot function without working technology. Having a reliable, dependable, fast, and fully functioning network for a district is critical. A technology outage can bring a school's operations to its knees. If you are not technology savvy, all the talk of networks, drivers, switches, routers, bandwidth, and system upgrades comes across like a foreign language. Having the right person in the position of technology director is crucial.

I have known directors who were brilliant with technology but could not communicate well with school employees. I have known directors who were exceptionally smart but had no idea how a school needed to run and just never fit into the education environment.

The best technology director I ever worked with was Amy Wood. Amy was a former teacher, worked in the curriculum department for a time, and was a technology guru. She could take any software, and after a short study time, have it figured out and installed, and then teach others to use it. Her knowledge of the technical side of the department was amazing, and she and her team diagnosed and fixed problems quickly, usually without anyone even knowing a problem existed. Her communication skills and down-to-earth relationships with district staff made her well-respected and liked, and hers was always a top-rated department in any survey we sent out.

One issue with educational technology is finding employees who have the skills necessary to do the job but also the understanding of education and how critical it is that our system be up and running at all times. As network managers, technicians, and systems operators mostly have backgrounds in technology but not education, it is key to hire the right mix of people to make up your technology department.

It is helpful to have technology-minded teachers working in the technology department as instructional specialists. They can go out and work directly with teachers to show them how to use software, explain it in a nonthreatening way, and even help teachers come up with sample lessons they can use immediately in the classroom. This approach leaves the technicians mainly in the background, doing what they like to do—focus on keeping systems operational.

In calendar planning, we typically required our entire staff to take the week of Independence Day as part of their vacation. We specified that during this week, no staff was to be on any district-owned technology or to access district software during that time, not even from home. We dedicated this week for our technology department to take the system down for upgrades, software updates, and any other technology-related issues that might otherwise disrupt school operations. By doing this, we kept our network robust and up to date, avoiding disruptions during times when our staff needed reliable technology most.

The technology department goes largely unnoticed when everything is running smoothly, and this should be the goal of any technology director. The best technology departments keep the network and systems dependable and working properly with almost no disruptions. Technology technicians working behind the scenes, and instructional specialists working with teachers to maximize technology in the classroom, make up the backbone of the department. The combination of these two specialties, along with a director who has a pulse on the department and can communicate clearly with school leadership, makes for a well-oiled machine that is a valuable asset to the entire district.

WHAT I LEARNED FROM LARRY BENNETT: ACKNOWLEDGE HARD WORK.

Dr. Bennett was my superintendent in Coldspring-Oakhurst CISD. He was a baseball fan and loved the fact that I was being brought in to build a baseball program. I inherited a horrible baseball facility, and I spent many hours working on my field after football practice and on weekends. I was attempting to make this field into something my players could be proud of and spent a lot of my time trying to make it happen.

After a few months of work, with Dr. Bennett periodically checking in on my progress, he called me into his office. "Jim, I know you have been killing yourself on that field, and

I just don't think you are going to have any luck getting new grass to grow on that field," he said. "The soil is not right, and all those hours you have spent on the tractor are just not getting it done. I just wanted you to know that you are going to have an eighteen-wheeler pull up to your field next week, and we are going to sod your entire infield."

Now, that may not sound like much, but for me, it was the world. He had acknowledged that I was going above and beyond for my players, and I wanted them to have a field they could be proud of. Despite my best efforts, I wasn't singlehandedly getting it done. With my new sod and an extra heavy seeding of winter ryegrass, when my players showed up for their first practice and saw their new field, it helped jumpstart the program's turnaround.

When department staffers know leadership supports them and will do things they don't have to do, it means a lot. That money wasn't in the athletic budget. It wasn't cheap, and I know Dr. Bennett had to pull those funds from some other pot of money. But when he did that, I knew he supported me and appreciated my hard work. I looked up to Dr. Bennett, and his acknowledging my hard work made me even more loyal to him.

Chapter Eleven

HANDLING THE UNEXPECTED WITH GRACE AND FINESSE

"Anyone can steer the ship when the winds are calm."

—PUBLILIUS SYRUS

NO MATTER YOUR EXPERIENCE, YOUR PREPARATION, OR your time on the job, unexpected incidents come up that you are not prepared for. You can be having a great year, and then your high school burns down overnight or a tornado takes out several campuses. You could have a random lightning strike kill an athlete on the playing field. School shootings, widespread flu, and pandemics are never expected. How you handle these times of extreme emotion—and potential panic from students, staff, and parents—is extremely important.

When I was a high school principal in a Northeast Texas school, I was out visiting with students in our outdoor commons area during lunch. After a few minutes, we all heard what sounded like an explosion coming from our agriculture building, which was located one hundred yards or so from our main building. I immediately ran in the direction of the explosion to see what had happened. As I approached a group of kids huddled around one of their classmates, they said, "Mr. Largent, he's been shot!"

I later learned a recent graduate had come to the agriculture shop to show the students and teacher a deer he had killed that morning. For some reason, he decided it was necessary to show the kids the gun he shot it with. The high-powered rifle was behind his seat, on the floorboard, with the barrel pointed toward the driver's side. The owner of the gun grabbed the barrel to pull it out and show the students, who were standing around his truck. As he pulled the gun from behind the seat, the trigger snagged on a hook attached to the seat and caused the loaded gun to fire. The bullet struck a student who was standing beside the owner and waiting to see the gun. It was a freak accident that the gun went off, but horrible and potentially deadly judgment by the owner of the gun.

I approached my student, who was on the ground and clearly in shock. He kept repeating, "I don't want to die. I don't want to die!" At that point, his health was my only concern. As I had first-aid training in my years as an athletic trainer, I evaluated my student for injuries. He had been shot in the groin area at the crease where his hip joint attached to his femur. This is an area that contains major arteries, and if that bullet had hit a major artery, I was going to have a dead high school student on my hands in a very short time. Other adults now on the scene moved everyone back and concealed my student from public view with a strategically placed blanket. After exposing the area where he had been shot, it was obvious the bullet had entered his hip and exited out his backside. It was a clean shot, but luckily there was no gushing blood, and that meant there was a chance the bullet did not hit an artery.

Emergency teams were en route, and until they arrived, I applied firm pressure on the entrance and exit wounds, trying my best to calm down my student. I heard that the emergency teams would not come to the scene of the shooting until they had identified the shooter and knew the situation was safe. After confirming there was no random shooter loose on our campus, emergency teams arrived, and a helicopter soon followed to transport the injured student to a hospital. Luckily, he survived and had a full recovery.

In high-stress situations, people observe how the leader is handling the situation. We do not plan for incidents like this. But when they happen, you have to respond accordingly. If the person in charge is running around yelling, screaming at people, and ranting about something they can't control, it doesn't help the situation. When I was a coach, I was fiery and vocal, and my competitive spirit showed. When I became an administrator, I learned this demeanor does not work well in high-stress situations, so I adjusted. To temper a situation, no matter how volatile, allows everything to slow down. When people see that their leader is calm, it has a calming effect on everyone. The calm space allows you to consider possible scenarios, consult with your team, and make good, clear decisions that are not based on emotion. When in doubt, even in the most stressful situations, slow down, chill out, and make well-thought-out decisions. The people you lead are watching.

POLITICS

No book about commonsense leadership in schools would be complete without a section on politics. Unfortunately, politics has infiltrated almost all parts of our society, and public schools are not exempt. I was the superintendent in a suburban area with a state representative who was a far-right politician. If there was a right-wing conspiracy theory, he believed it. Anything anyone said within a variety of right-wing internet groups was the gospel truth, according to him.

He was speaking to a Republican women's group in our town and verbally attacked my character! He told the group my salary had increased more than 50 percent over the last five years but that teachers had not received a raise during that time. Someone in attendance relayed this information to me. This was a complete lie, as our teachers had received a raise every year I was at the school, and my salary certainly had not doubled.

I texted the representative, asking if he had indeed said these untruths. His response was a screenshot of a report from an out-of-state right-wing "think tank" known for attacking public schools. The report was filled with completely false information, the kind of nonsense some politicians spew in communities across our country. If left unchecked, they continue to spread misinformation because it serves as red meat to their constituents and benefits them politically.

As you think about politics, there are a few areas where leaders need to lead! Too many leaders are scared of getting involved, so they avoid the topic, let politicians say anything they want, or worse, treat them as if they are special when they show up for photo ops at schools. This brings me to my first topic related to politics—voting.

VOTING

What would you say if your governor announced they were going to poll 3 percent of the state's population on major decisions, and whatever that 3 percent says, they were going to do? That 3 percent would decide the future of your state. My guess is that you would be incensed. What about the other 97 percent of us and our views? Aren't we important? Don't we deserve to be heard? Surely we can't allow this to happen!

Regretfully, in the current state of politics, this is exactly what is happening. In many states, a single political party controls the politics while the other party has virtually no chance of winning a statewide election. In these states, most statewide election decisions are made in the primaries.

For an illustration, let's look at the 2014 race for Texas lieutenant governor. In that race, 1.3 million people voted in the Republican primary, and Dan Patrick got just over 552,000 votes. That put him in a runoff election against David Dewhurst. In the runoff, only 750,000 people voted, and Patrick won with 489,000 votes. In 2014, there were more than 15.5 million eligible voters in Texas and more than 14 million registered voters. So, by doing the simple math, Dan Patrick was elected with just over 3 percent of eligible Texas voters casting their votes for him, and 97 percent of Texas citizens voted for someone else or didn't vote.

Unfortunately, a similar scenario plays out in every election cycle, with extremely low voter turnout and people left asking, "How in the world did this person get elected?" With the primary form of elections in most states, the real election is on primary night and not the general election. Historically, primaries bring out fringe voters on the extremes of each party, and the vast majority of people just don't vote. This is why we now see two parties on completely opposite ends of the political spectrum, and many of us ask how these crazies get elected. They get elected because extremists and radicals (in both parties) vote, while a huge majority of normal citizens sit out elections.

I constantly remind staff about the importance of voting. We need to be informed voters, not just falling in line with candidates who spend the most money or repeat a few national hot-topic issues we may agree with. We must do a little research, ask questions, and find out where candidates truly stand on important issues.

Again for illustrative purposes, there are over 1.3 million active and retired school employees in Texas, and if they all voted, we could easily elect candidates who place public education and students at the top of their priorities. Instead, we continue to see elected officials who publicly announce they are pushing major reform in public education, which usually means they want to divert tax dollars to private schools, add more useless bubble tests, or find more hoops for us to jump through under the guise of holding us accountable. The problem is that none of these ideas proves to be anything new and never involves the expertise of professional educators. Most lack any proven research, and almost none would actually help children. We allow people who have never walked a day in our shoes to trash us in public and tell us how we should do our jobs. Unbelievably, we still don't show up on Election Day, allowing this cycle to continue. By not voting, we elect people who want to do away with public education as we know it.

As leaders, it is part of our jobs to inform employees about elections and the importance of voting. If politicians knew 100 percent of educators were going to vote, you can bet they would support pro-public-education policies. It boggles my mind as to why an entire industry that could sway politics in the country does not do the easiest and most effective action they could do— *vote!*

NEW BREED OF CRAZY

Schools all over our nation are dealing with a new breed of crazy. The coronavirus pandemic has caused fringe groups to lose their minds over mask and vaccine mandates, social distancing, and many other policies or rules that schools put in place to try to combat this global health issue. Other issues that have turned ugly are the discussion of critical race theory (CRT) and a push to ban books from schools. As these issues have come around at virtually the same time, our country has witnessed some of the worst behavior possible from politicians, parents, political activists, and others who use schools as a platform to gain public exposure to promote their views over the views of others.

In an interim superintendency I did during the pandemic, a parent emailed my high school principal and called him a Nazi for following masking guidelines the CDC recommended, the state advocated for, and the school board voted on and approved. People called the office repeatedly to chastise us for the "far-left liberal" views they said we were indoctrinating our children with—all because we were following guidelines passed down from our federal and state government and actions taken by our locally elected school board. It is amazing that an issue such as a global health scare has drawn hatred from the left and the right. Are we in such a state of chaos that we can't even come together for the common purpose of saving lives?

The ugliness we have seen during the pandemic is part of the political "culture wars" we find ourselves in at this time in history. We have seen videos of people standing in front of their school boards, yelling and proclaiming the pandemic is a hoax. Human decency, respect for school officials, and basic decorum have been replaced by radical screaming matches that end with school officials and board members being threatened in the public square.

Critical race theory is another issue that has skyrocketed to the national spotlight. Honestly, if you had asked one thousand educators what CRT was, in 2020, most would have likely told you they had never heard of it and did not know what it was. What began as a "think tank" scholarly white paper at an Ivy League school in the 1970s has been transformed into a national issue for political gain. The narrative being peddled is that schools are teaching white people to be ashamed that they are white and that all Black people are victims.

In all my years in education, I did not participate in one conversation in which we discussed anything remotely like this. Are there examples of educators teaching inappropriate lessons in schools? Of course. Are there teachers who share this view and have said things in class that were inappropriate? Of course. Do these isolated issues rise to a level that should be the dog-whistle moment it has become for radicals? Of course not.

I am all for parents having access to information, asking questions, and being able to see what is being taught in schools. They certainly have that right, and all public schools have processes in place for parents, or any member of the public for that matter, to question virtually anything we do in our schools. Public information requests, grievance processes, and conferences with teachers, principals, or directors all provide parents the ability to learn practically anything they want about our schools.

So, how does a commonsense leader deal with this new breed of radical, whose only objective is to embarrass a school while shedding light on their own issue or radical thoughts? There are some commonsense ways to handle this, but it requires cooperation from your school board, law enforcement, and local judicial officials.

Set meeting norms and follow them. First I advise you to make sure any public meeting has a defined set of policies that are immediately enforced. A board meeting is for the school board to conduct the business of the school. It is not a public forum for political speeches on topics seen on some radical internet site. Attendees should know the decorum expected in the meeting as well as what they can or cannot do or say.

How long a person can speak, what topics they can speak on, the fact that they cannot publicly attack individuals, and making only general statements about a particular topic are all very common policies that should be in any school board policy book. Announce these policies with specifics about what will and will not be tolerated, before anyone is allowed to speak, for any meeting that has the potential for volatile speakers.

The real key is to have a school board president or presiding officer who will enforce these policies and immediately cut people off when they defy the rules. This is hard for some board members to do, and those who are unwilling to enforce their own policies are part of the reason these meetings get out of hand. Board officers must have a clear understanding of what is in the policy and immediately act when people stray from those policies.

Have law enforcement at meetings to enforce the law. It is a shame we are in a time when we need to have a law enforcement presence at a simple school board meeting. But that is where we are. Threats and verbal assaults unfortunately have become the norm in school board meetings all over our country. It should be required for school officials, and the law enforcement officers who will work the meetings, to meet and go over the policy and relevant laws. When a speaker at a podium makes a threat or otherwise does something illegal, they should be immediately removed from the meeting and, in some cases, arrested or issued a "no-trespass" citation that bans them from attending public meetings for a period of time.

Prosecute threats, and let it be known that this behavior will not be tolerated. The only way to stop the nonsense is to prosecute radicals for breaking the law. If a person makes a threat, they should be arrested and made to go through the legal proceedings to address that violation. If they disrupt a meeting, they should be issued a no-trespass citation that would not allow them on school property for a period of time.

Schools can get a handle on this tribe mentality at board meetings only by setting clear guidelines and policies for what is and is not allowed, enlisting the help of law enforcement to combat threats or unruly behavior, and having the legal system follow up.

SPEAK UP

The worst thing leaders can do is allow politicians to lie and misrepresent facts to the public. I have seen it time and again. Many school leaders don't want to get involved in politics or think it will do no good, but somebody has to stand up for our students and staff. If you won't do it, who will?

You don't have to pick a fight with your local politicians, but they should be held accountable for their votes and what they say in public. It incenses me when politicians vote for laws that hurt our schools but show up for every photo opportunity with our students. When someone lies about the organization I am in charge of, I will correct the record! Emailing staff, giving quotes to local media outlets, and correcting misinformation in newsletters and board meetings are all ways to combat lies from politicians and their cohorts. Unfortunately, too few school leaders are willing to stand up and correct elected leaders. This is a problem that will get worse if we don't act!

INFORMING STAFF AND THE PUBLIC

I used my weekly email to inform my staff on legislation and politics that affected our schools. While never telling my staff who to vote for, I felt it was my job to inform them about how our elected leaders had voted on matters pertaining to education. A local senator in one district where I worked was a really nice guy— personable, seen in public quite a bit, and well-liked. But when it came to vouchers or other issues that hurt public schools, he always voted right along with the party leader, and most of his votes were considered anti public education.

When we were in a legislative session, I made a point each week to let my staff know how our state representative and senator had voted on key legislation. If they voted for vouchers or some other legislation that took away local control, I let my staff know. If they voted for something that helped us, I let them know that as well. My goal was to inform staff on what was going on at the capitol, for those who were not paying attention.

THE CHALLENGE

My challenge for you is to find creative ways to inform your staff and the public on how your politicians are doing. Call out their lies, correct them when they claim to misunderstand, and publicize their votes on key education issues. Somehow we have to get back to voting for people and not parties, electing people who support students and staff. I challenge you to be a bold leader and become known for holding politicians accountable for their actions after they are elected.

PROMOTE VOTING

As I have said, voting is the number one thing that can solve many problems in education. Groups like Texans for Public Education rate candidates and report their support, or lack of support, for public schools. This group is also building a coalition of people who pledge to vote for the best candidates, not based on party affiliation. Imagine a country where elected officials knew that without the support of the education community, they could never win an election. Imagine a country where 99 percent of people who work in education in any capacity voted in every election for candidates who support public education above all other political issues. Imagine what our schools would look like if there were a national push to make public schools the best they could possibly be and give every child an opportunity to succeed, no matter their ethnicity, socioeconomic level, or zip code. Just imagine what changes would sweep across our country if we elected people who shared those views. Just imagine...

THE MEDIA

I pride myself on being able to get along and work with almost anyone. I try to have a very transparent relationship with reporters, and in fact, I've had very good relations with almost every reporter and newspaper staffer I've ever dealt with. It's good to build solid relationships with people who write about and interview you over the course of your tenure.

Leaders in education should make every effort to be open and honest with media professionals, and hopefully, reporters will understand that lines have to be drawn sometimes regarding what you can or cannot say—and what they should or should not write. Journalists have a job to do and content to distribute, and they need stories to feed that beast. By the same token, I expect them to be fair and allow me to have a say on controversial issues, knowing they will print views from all sides of a situation. If you can establish boundaries, it is normally very easy to have a productive and enjoyable relationship with local media.

When I was in a small town with a newspaper that came out only twice a week, I regularly fed them information that would come out later in the week. With the popularity of social media and today's instant news cycle, papers that don't put out a new edition daily are in a bind. By the time their weekend edition is public, most of the area news is already considered old news. This can hamper a local paper's operations, so anytime I could help, I did.

I had a great relationship with my local editor and education reporter. It was so good, in fact, that I hand-delivered press releases about upcoming staff changes or issues worthy of front-page news. A couple of times, staff members were going to be arrested or a major personnel change was pending, and I let editors know what was coming so they could be ready to print the story when the information became public.

By doing this, I established trust, and reporters regularly called to ask about rumors or verify information they heard on the street. If the rumors were true, I confirmed, and if they were false or I had no knowledge, I told them so. Because we had this mutual trust, if a particular situation warranted a little more time behind the scenes, I could ask them to delay the story. Most of the time, they allowed me to do my job before they made it public. In another school district, I ran into a different kind of education reporter, an experience not nearly as cordial. This newspaper's style was similar to the *National Enquirer*. Instead of focusing on our school's successes by filling their paper with photos of kids playing sports and feel-good stories from the community, their reporters focused on digging up dirt and trying to embarrass or shed a bad light on our school and other areas of our community. I never understood this local newspaper's strategy. As the new superintendent to the district, this floored me. I had never dealt with a local newspaper whose goal was to damage its community.

Over the next couple of years, many events occurred that completely turned me off. First, the paper's editorial staff basically demanded we send them our board agenda with supporting documents several days before it was required to go public. Then, they published a few interviews and related stories in their weekend edition ahead of the Monday board meeting. Most stories were negative and tended to provoke the community about some policy, tax rate, or other issues to be discussed at the board meeting. For some reason, the prior administration had gone along with these editors' demands, despite their negative impact on the school.

Next, the editors ran negative articles about the district without reaching out to school personnel for comment. They printed pictures taken by our school photographer and did not credit him for the photos. An editorial section invited anyone to go to the newspaper's website and submit anonymous messages to an online forum. Community members bashed local businesses, schools, coaches, or anyone else, and some were printed in the paper, with no fact-checking. One year, my salary was the front-page headline, in huge numbers, obviously an attempt to ridicule me and some of my administrative team.

They showed up at civic functions, where I gave speeches, and even though 99 percent of my speech was positive, these reporters picked out a single sentence or two and twisted it into something negative and completely out of context. It was so bad that we canceled the school's subscription to the paper. The newspaper was a mill for people who craved gossip over real news. It became a local joke of a publication because of how bad it was.

I had to develop a strategy to turn this around, and I knew it would be difficult because I was the new guy in town. I arranged a meeting with the local editor to discuss my concerns. At this point, he was not too interested in what I had to say. I think because he had been allowed to bully former superintendents, he assumed I would go along with whatever he wanted. Next, I wrote a letter to the owner of the newspaper, complaining about the anonymous gossip column each week and citing specific articles I thought were unfair. Sending this letter to the owner of the paper did not go over well with the local editor, so the situation actually got worse. It was time for the next level of engagement.

In local government, we have to follow laws regarding open records. Essentially, anyone can request any record from the school, and school officials have to produce the requested record. This may be test scores, salary information, contracts with personnel or vendors, and basically any other record related to operating the school. But people who make those requests have to do so in writing, and timelines associated with the requests allow a reasonable amount of time to produce the documents. Normally, a request must be fulfilled within ten days, but if it requires clarification, is deemed classified, or involves large volumes, the process can be delayed or fees can be assessed.

Also, as part of the Open Records Act, we don't have to produce documents we don't have, we don't have to answer a list of questions, and we don't have to compile information for the requester. For instance, if a reporter wants a list of all the property in the district worth over five million dollars, we may not have a report for that. But we have a list of all the properties in the district and their values. So, if a person requests the information, they may get a list of every property in the school district. Then, they would have to scour through the list to find the property values. I'm sure you see where I am going with this.

After trying our best to work with our local newspaper reporters and editors without any success, we employed another tactic. No law says school personnel have to agree to interviews with local reporters. No law says coaches have to send outcome reports for ball games. Nothing says we have to send the local paper any information before it is made public. So, we stopped being overly cooperative with our local newspaper. Such drastic measures are advisable only as a last resort. So, when reasonable efforts proved unsuccessful, we began delaying district information to the local newspaper and distributed our news via other channels.

If a reporter made a request for an interview, we declined. If the newspaper sent over a series of questions for us to answer, we treated it as an Open Records request and sent only documents that might answer the question. And we took our time to respond, while still following the law. If a reporter asked a question and we did not have a document to support it, we told them, "Sorry, but we don't possess any document that pertains to your request." If they wanted scores from ball games, they had to send a reporter to games. We informed editorial staff that they needed to submit a written request before using any photo from our website, and credit to our photographer was required if reprint permission was granted. We played hardball!

We let parents and community members know that for up-to-date information about our schools, they should subscribe to our weekly email, Facebook page, and Twitter feed. We emailed a weekly wrap-up of all school-related news, and people could opt in or out. Each sport had its own feed, so if a baseball fan wanted only baseball scores, they could subscribe just to that feed.

We mailed and emailed letters to every contact we had, to let them know that if they wanted the latest news from our school, this was where to find it. Our goal was to make our local newspaper useless to our community as it related to news about our schools, and it worked. This predictably infuriated our local newspaper editors.

Our information delay lasted the better part of a year. I know the local editor was getting pressure from the owner as subscriptions dropped, layoffs and financial cutbacks occurred, and the paper became a bare-bones publication. There was virtually no news to report from our school in our local newspaper. Their having to file an Open Records request for every story about our school was certainly not sustainable for them.

After our months-long standoff, the editor called me and asked for another meeting. We met in my office and had a long conversation about all that concerned me about the negative articles. The editor seemed to want to start over. I told him I knew his staff had a job to do but that I wished reporters would be fairer with our school and, more importantly, give our kids the publicity they deserved. The anonymous gossip column was discontinued, and reporters began writing more positive stories about our school. We slowly opened up access, again responding to questions and interview requests. In the end, we made it work and traded our tremendously toxic interactions for a relationship that was never perfect but remained cordial. Years later, a well-liked local businessman bought the paper and turned the publication into the hometown newspaper it should have been all along.

In today's social media culture, nearly any story that makes a front-page headline is already well circulated. Community newspapers that release only one or two editions per week might better serve readers by becoming "feel-good" publications, featuring positive stories about the community and including lots of photos of smiling school kids.

SELF-HELP AND STRESS RELIEF

The job of a school leader is stressful! You are on call 24/7, 365. If a school burns down on Christmas Eve, you are going to work. If a school tragedy happens while you're on a long-planned vacation, you will get a call. Even though your contract may say you work 226 days or 240 days annually, in reality, you are always on call.

As a cool, calm, and collected leader (except during my coaching career), I felt that my stress level remained relatively low most of the time. But after I retired, so many people came up to me and made comments such as "I can see retirement is being good to you" and "You just look so stress-free." Even though I was never one to rant and rave, yell, or get too worked up, I guess my stress level was obvious to those around me.

In a stressful job like school leadership, taking care of yourself has to be a top priority. Superintendents spend so much time worrying about and taking care of board members, employees, and students that we sometimes forget about ourselves. Countless books, articles, and research studies are related to managing stress, so I won't go into a long discussion about that here, but there are a few key things to help drive down stress levels:

Exercise. Of all the things we can do, a regular exercise routine may be the most important. I have been in a habit for most of my life of doing something active virtually every day. Walking, swimming, biking, strength training, and engaging in sports like golf, pickleball, and basketball are some ways I stay active. If you love certain activities, make them a part of your daily life. Choose an activity you look forward to and can do long term. Being physical is so ingrained in my daily life that I just don't feel right unless I get my exercise in.

More than the physiological reasons for exercise, just taking some time to focus on something healthy is a main benefit. When I ride my bike or play a round of golf, a calmness comes over me. I find myself taking in the details of nature, flowers, colors, and sounds of my surroundings. Sometimes I listen to audiobooks to take my mind to another place while I exercise.

Everyone is different, but before I retired, morning was the only time I could find to consistently exercise. By the time my day was over, some event after school, meetings, or the need for family time interfered with an evening routine. I found that if I got up an hour or so early, I could get my exercise done, and it just made me feel so much better. Whatever works for you is fine, but a consistent habit of physical exercise is beneficial beyond measure.

Leave it at work. Another helpful way to alleviate stress is to leave your problems at work! That is easier said than done, but a conscious effort helps immensely. Working ten or more hours a day in a stressful environment, then coming home and talking about it with your spouse or family for another two hours after work, is not healthy. It only serves to maintain an already elevated stress level.

Many of the most stressed leaders don't have hobbies or activities outside of work, so they spend all their time, even at home, thinking about and worrying about work-related issues. It is imperative to take your mind off work when you get home. Reading, sports, learning new skills, woodworking, restoring cars, refinishing furniture, yoga, and meditation are activities that can take your mind to a completely different place—away from work.

Build a great team. Surrounding yourself with people you trust, respect, and work well with can have a huge impact on your daily work life and stress levels. A huge stress reliever for a leader is knowing you can immediately call your cabinet or an administrative team to talk through issues before making key decisions.

Unfortunately, in dysfunctional teams, the leader often makes decisions without consulting anyone and leaves his colleagues wondering why he made the decisions. If a team is apprehensive because they never know when a leader is going to snap, yell, or act irrationally, few people are willing to risk being berated if they speak up.

At the end of the day, stress relief and taking care of oneself is a huge part of success. Daily exercise, taking your mind off work with hobbies and skills, and leaving work issues at work are all ways to cut stress. Find what works for you. What are your interests? What do you enjoy doing? Stressful moments come with any job, but some simple strategies can mitigate stress to improve your work and home life. Stress doesn't have to come with success!

GREAT EXPECTATIONS

I grew up primarily in the '60s and '70s, graduated high school in 1983, and am immensely proud of how I was raised. My parents worked hard all their lives to provide the best environment they could for my brother, John, and me. Mom and Dad both worked for the local school district, and my dad took on second and third jobs, started businesses, and tinkered with or built items to make a little extra money.

The biggest impact of my upbringing is that my parents instilled in me a work ethic and motivation to excel. If I started something, I finished it. If I participated in a sport, club, or any other organization, I wanted to lead and be the best at it. I certainly never achieved my goal of being the best at everything, but I was willing to do extra work, practice more, or go above what was expected to give anything my best shot. I hated to fail (still do) and was motivated by my parents' expectations of me. Their subtle leadership, capped with high expectations, discipline, and not accepting failure, was an early lesson for me on commonsense leadership. I took what I learned from my parents and carried that over to my career.

Bonus Chapter

THE BLUEPRINT FOR SECURING AND SUCCEEDING ON YOUR WAY TO THE TOP

THROUGHOUT THIS BOOK IS A SERIES OF STRATEGIES I call commonsense leadership. I hope you have enjoyed the stories, the situations, and the reasoning behind my suggestions. Now, I want to show you how to put it all together, from determining your career path to applying for the job—and the first things to do when you land that job.

I approach this chapter as if you are seeking a position as a superintendent in a school district, guiding you through the steps to take as you plan this career move. You can adjust some of these steps if you are moving into a different leadership position, such as principal or director, but much of my advice still applies.

ADMINISTRATIVE CAREER PATHS

When journeying along a career path in education, some people are motivated by money, others by position, and many others by geography and family considerations. Acknowledging several factors early in a career can lay some groundwork as you move forward:

Money

Money is a great motivator, and while it shouldn't be the reason for getting into any line of work, there is nothing wrong with expecting fair compensation for what you do. Nothing is wrong with searching for opportunities that pay well if the situation is right for you and your family. If you do a great job, people will hear about you, and that comes with opportunities for growth, career moves, and increased compensation.

A finding from my dissertation years ago was that those who moved a little more often and pursued jobs at larger districts made more money. That seems like common sense, but I recommend to board members that when you find the perfect superintendent for a district, offer a pay rate that keeps them happy and in your school. People approach successful superintendents about other opportunities, which often come with better perks, a larger district, more staff, and a bigger salary. Paying a few thousand dollars extra to keep a successful superintendent is money well spent.

I was never one to move just to chase money, and I was lucky I had school boards that wanted to keep my compensation package competitive. For my part, each year during my evaluation and contract review, I provided my board with salaries of area super-intendents at similar-size schools, and if they asked, I told them what I thought was a fair salary for the upcoming year.

Don't be shy about compensation. I've seen superintendents turn down raises or tell the board they are happy with their salary as a symbolic show of loyalty. When things go south, I have seen many school boards cut off the limb while a superintendent is hanging on the end, and a once good relationship ends quickly. My advice is to never turn down a raise, and always ask for your compensation to be competitive with peers. You have an obligation to yourself and your family to be fairly compensated for tremendously hard and stressful work.

Geography

Studies show a large percentage of people live within a fifty-mile radius of where they were raised. In education, this is very common. If you are determined to live within a certain geography because of family or because you simply like the pine trees, rivers, lakes, mountains, or desert, good for you. Just know that when you set these parameters, you limit your options for advancement.

Everyone has their reasons for where they want to live, and I get it. But, if you are trying to advance your career, especially if opportunities are not there for you, consider expanding the geographic regions in which you are willing to work. Seeing how people in other areas live and work is fun. While I have been in Texas my entire career, I have worked in deep East Texas, the Houston area, the far northeast corner of Texas, and out to the upper hill country west of Fort Worth. I have found that while climates are a little different, communities have different cultures, and the sizes of schools are different, the kids in the classroom are mostly the same at their core.

In my study, educators who chose to stay in a particular school district or area were most likely to get their first superintendent job later in life. They normally got into a district they liked, stayed, and worked their way up the administrative chain of command, eventually becoming superintendent. But it usually took a long time to achieve that ultimate goal. There is absolutely nothing wrong with staying an entire career in the same district, but understand how that may affect your career path and the length of time to reach your goals.

I am one of the lucky ones who enjoyed every place I ever worked. I have friends and colleagues all over the country; have experienced cultural, economic, and ethnic diversity; and have gone from the high heat and humidity of East Texas to the drier heat and cool evenings in the upper hill country.

Position

Ever since I was a child, I wanted to be the leader of whatever team or group I was involved in. I wanted to be pitcher, quarterback, and class president, and when I got into the school business, I was motivated to become head coach, high school principal, and ultimately superintendent. I learned as much as I could along the way, but when I thought I was ready for that next career move, I went for it.

It is challenging to prepare for leadership jobs in education. No one can prepare you for a crazy parent or disgruntled staff member or lunatic community member. I have had to rely on common sense in almost every new position. Sure, experience helps, and having good mentors who talk you through situations is extremely valuable, but until you are in the seat, doing the work, you can never be truly prepared. One more year as a principal or two more as an assistant superintendent doesn't fully prepare you for the superintendency, in my opinion.

My dissertation from years ago included some interesting findings about the tenures of superintendents. Longer-tenured superintendents tended to be in smaller schools, made less money, and were likely hired with a school board doing the search. Higher-paid superintendents tended to have shorter tenure, served larger schools, and were often hired in schools that used search consultants.

Unless you have specific reasons for not leaving an area, consider expanding your horizons if career advancement is a top priority. You may have to take a job in an unfamiliar place. Remember, you can always move again!

WHAT I LEARNED FROM JIMMY MERCHANT: TAKE LEAPS OF FAITH.

When I enrolled at Sam Houston State University to finish my master's work, one of my first professors was Dr. Jimmy Merchant. We immediately hit it off, and he became my mentor throughout my time at Sam Houston. Dr. Merchant was from a small town in Northeast Texas and had worked in public schools for a time, and he and I seemed to have a lot in common. He was easy to talk to, he did not have the attitude or ego some professors have, and I think he liked me as much as I liked him.

Dr. Merchant came to me in the spring of 1995 and told me about an opening for high school principal in a town not far from where he grew up. He knew the superintendent and had already called him on my behalf. He and I talked about my chances of making a jump from assistant principal to principal with only a couple of years' experience, and Dr. Merchant was confident I could do it. After going through the interview process, I became a high school principal and left the coaching profession earlier than I had planned to pursue school administration.

Several years later, Dr. Merchant and I reunited when I applied for and was accepted to become a member of the third cohort of doctoral students at Sam Houston State. Dr. Merchant continued to mentor me, became the chair of my dissertation committee, and always supported me in my endeavors.

APPLYING FOR AND INTERVIEWING FOR JOBS

After hiring literally hundreds of people throughout the course of my career, I have seen common themes from people who get the job and from those who don't. When applying for a job, the first bit of commonsense advice is to apply only for jobs for which you are qualified. I have seen elementary physical education teachers apply for head football jobs, people with no high school or administrative experience apply to be high school principals at 5A schools, and middle school teachers apply for superintendent jobs. Be ambitious but realistic about your career ambitions. While it is fine to dream and keep lofty goals, do not waste people's time by applying for jobs when you are clearly not qualified.

Assuming you are qualified for the job, your immediate goal is to get an interview. The biggest hurdle when applying for a job is to actually get in the door. Find ways to set yourself apart from other candidates, to make your application stand out.

Write a cover letter. Most districts now use digital media for the application process. If you are applying online for a job, find a way to make your application stand out if at all possible. Various colors, bold letters, different fonts, and images all attract a little more attention to your application. If you are submitting hard copies of your application and resume, use a high-quality, slightly different colored paper. I always bought heavy cotton paper, slightly tan in color. If nothing else, in a stack of virtually all white paper, mine looked a little different.

The cover letter is not a lengthy document, maybe a page or two at most. The sweet spot is a letter about a page and a half in length. If you want to condense as much information as possible into a small space, structure a cover letter as follows: 1) In the first paragraph, give a general introduction of yourself, your current position, and why you are interested in the job. 2) Next, give a brief list of reasons why you are a good fit for the position. If you have any connection to the school or community, include that in your letter. 3) Then relay your enthusiasm about the job prospect and how eager you are to meet and talk about the position.

Write the letter in such a way that the reader can feel your excitement, your interest in the job, and the fact that you are more than qualified and ready for the challenge the job offers. The last paragraph should be worded in a way that lets the hiring team know you expect to be called for an interview: *I look forward to meeting with you in person and talking more about my qualifications and enthusiasm about the job.* Your cover letter should be concise, energetic, and well-written, inspiring hiring teams to want to meet you as soon as possible.

Draft a resume. Let me dispel a rumor about resumes. Anyone who tells you a resume should be only one page is wrong! Maybe if you are a teenager applying to work at the local fast food restaurant, that will suffice, but if you are applying for a professional position, the people reviewing your resume want a clear picture of your experience, achievements, education, key leadership positions, and evidence that you have been an asset to your employers' organizations. That requires more than one sheet of paper. The resume is a crucial piece of the application process. A poor resume turns off the reader, no matter your qualifications. Simple mistakes like a misspelled word, referencing the wrong school, gaps in employment, or a poorly formatted document can keep you from getting an interview. A properly formatted resume follows a fairly standard order:

- **Personal Information:** At the top, place your full name and contact information, including an email address and phone number where you can be reached.

- **Formal Education:** The next section should outline your formal education, starting with your latest school and degree at the top, then working through other schools and degrees as you go.

- **Relevant Certifications:** Include a section for certifications and any special training you have received. This is where you can list your mid-management or superintendent certification. You might also list other endorsements that make you stand out—maybe you are a mentor superintendent or a TEA-registered provider for board and administrator training. If you are a national trainer for some type of professional development, state that here. This section highlights additional skills that are not part of your formal degree program.

- **Employment History:** Outline your job history in chronological order from present to previous, including where you worked, the years you were employed there, and the position you held. List all professional jobs after college in this section, preferably with no gaps in employment. If there is a two-year gap between jobs, people will usually ask why. If you took a two-year sabbatical to work in the Peace Corp or explore Europe, that is fine, but put that information in the resume to fill the gap.

- **Areas of Expertise:** On your resume, have a section that lists specific skillsets. For me, it was team-building, authentic learning, and planning and supervising building projects. If you are an expert in school finance or have had particular success with school turnarounds, showcase it here. Do some research on the school to which you are applying and highlight your expertise with areas in which they may be in need. If the school is about to go into a huge bond program, cite "bond planning" as one of your strengths. If the district has several low-performing schools, cite your track record for increasing academic success.

- **Continuing Studies:** People want to see that you take advantage of additional learning opportunities, so if you have been part of a select group of people to go to a full-year learning institute, list it. Maybe you were part of a group that studied schools in impoverished areas as part of a corporate scholarship for school leaders. List that. Did you voluntarily pay your own way to attend an aspiring leadership academy over the summer? List that, too. Anything that shows you are going above and beyond to prepare for your next positions is impressive.

- **Leadership Positions:** Maybe you serve on the board of the local chamber of commerce, youth sports leagues, or the local Lions or Kiwanis Club. Most schools, when hiring their new leader, want to know you will be involved in the community outside of school, so this is a good place to show you are active and involved.

- **Awards and Honors:** If you have received special awards during your professional career, cite them. Being named teacher or principal of the year, competitive scholarships you received to pay for your master's degree, and other prestigious awards or honors should go in this section. If you were a Green Beret in the military, completed an internship in the White House, or are an Eagle Scout, you should be especially proud of those achievements, so share them with your prospective employer. They might be impressed, and if someone reading your resume just happens to be an Eagle Scout or former Green Beret, that small bit of information might get you in the door for an interview!

- **Professional Affiliations:** Cite professional organizations of which you are a member, for example, if you are actively involved in an administrators association, writers' association, or storytelling guild.

- **References:** I consider this an addendum to the actual resume, but when I applied for jobs, I always included it. My reference section sometimes changed depending on the job I was applying for. This is not customary, but I included a short description of my relationship to the person. For example, if I cited Dr. Chester Juroska as a reference, I gave his contact information and then wrote, "Dr. Juroska was my superintendent while I served as a high school principal in Queen City ISD. He was instrumental in my career and encouraged me to become a superintendent." Another tip for references is to include a variety of people, not just colleagues or supervisors—a board president or two, local businesspeople, the chamber of commerce president, bankers, and maybe a mayor if I had those connections. Always contact the people on your reference sheet to let them know they may be contacted, and also to make sure their contact information is current.

You may or may not need in your job application to provide your curriculum vitae (CV), or just vitae. In the scholarly world, the vitae is a detailed list of your professional accomplishments. This includes achievements in each position you have held, speeches you have given, honors and awards attained, articles or books written, and generally a backward chronology of your professional life. This can be quite lengthy and is not always necessary when applying for a job. However, I always included it in case the interviewer wanted a more detailed view of my professional history.

One other tip: attach a professional picture of yourself, or of you and your family, to the front page of your resume. In today's digital world, you can easily add a photo to your resume, and this can be a positive addition for several reasons. One, it puts a face with a name, which is always good. Two, if you have school-age kids, it lets people who are reviewing resumes know you are likely bringing your own kids to the district, which is usually looked upon favorably. Physical appearance shouldn't affect hiring decisions, but knowing, for instance, that a young family is moving to a community may be positive in some cases.

My final piece of advice is to make your resume, reference sheet, and CV a working document. These should be updated regularly and kept current. Anytime something significant happens in your career, add it to your resume or CV, and you will always have up-to-date information ready to go when opportunities arise. I keep my resume current even today.

Make personal contacts. Making personal contacts or having others call on your behalf is somewhat controversial. But if I am in search of a superintendent, and a respected colleague calls to tell me someone is worthy of an interview, I listen! If you are tight with someone associated with the school, consider enlisting them to help you get in the door. But I suggest some parameters.

First, don't call board members unless you know them personally or they ask you to call them. I do think it is helpful to call the outgoing superintendent, unless there is some scandal about their departure. It amazed me, as a sitting superintendent, that when I announced I was leaving and my job was open, very few people called me to ask about the position. I know some were being respectful of my time, others didn't think they should call, and some didn't want to take the time. But done correctly, it can help you get an interview. In two of my three superintendent jobs, the former superintendents told me I was the only applicant who called and spoke to them about the job. They relayed that information to the board members. It definitely didn't hurt, since I got those jobs!

Don't bombard a search consultant with calls, but if you can get two or three well-respected people to call on your behalf, I promise it will help you get in the door. If a consultant hears your name several times from well-respected people, they become curious about you and want to learn more. When I began my path to becoming a superintendent, I called and set up meetings with the top search consultants at the time. I wanted them to know me personally and made sure they could put a face with a name when I applied for their jobs. I believe these meetings paid dividends for me. Your main objective at this stage of the process is to get an interview! If you don't get an interview, you can't get the job.

THE INTERVIEW

Once you are granted an interview, the real work begins. From interviewing hundreds of people, I can tell you what works and what is a real turnoff to interview teams. Doing the proper research and planning before your interview gives you the best chance at moving forward in the process.

The mistake I see most with a lot of applicants is the failure to research the place where they are applying to work. If you haven't taken the time to thoroughly research a job, you don't deserve to get it! In many interviews, we would ask a candidate to tell us what they knew about the school, and they couldn't. They didn't know even basic information such as the campus location or how many students were enrolled. This was an instant turnoff to me, and I guarantee it will be to most interview committees.

When you go into an interview for a leadership position, know as much as possible about the job and the organization: *Where is the building located? How many staff members work there? How many students attend? What are the campus ratings and why? What are significant data points that stand out to you as a professional? Are there problems with student attendance or staff turnover? What is something unique about the school that you've noticed or heard about?* All of this information is readily available, so do your homework and be prepared.

To prepare for job interviews, I made simple notes and took them with me to the interview. I always brought a nice, professional leather notebook with me so I could also take notes during the interview. But on the left side of that notebook was a little cheat sheet I could quickly refer to if needed. Most of the time, I had read over the information enough times that I didn't even have to look at it, but it was there if I needed it.

If you know more about their school than they do, you'll have a big advantage in the interview. I have been in several interviews where I mentioned something about the district and noticed the board members looking at one another with raised eyebrows and a little smirk. I had just told them something they didn't know about their school. Those board members were thinking, *If a stranger can walk into a room full of people affiliated with the district for years and tell us something we don't know, what could they do for us if they were to work here full time?* Do your homework! It pays off.

How you structure your responses to questions is of utmost importance. Remember these four words: *It's not about me!* By the time you get into the interview, the people in the room do not care so much about your awards, how wonderful your last job was, or your staff's love for you. They are interested in one thing— what you can do for them! Knowing that, go into the interview prepared to talk about their school. My next tip is to give thorough but concise answers. You are giving the interview team a snapshot of you and your leadership style. Nothing is worse for an interview team than asking a simple question and having to listen for the next twenty minutes while the applicant gives a sermon. The interview team is likely interviewing quite a few people for this job, and if you are confident, excited, and concise with your answers, you will stand out. I always told the interview team during my introductory statement that I was going to be concise and to the point, but if they wanted me to elaborate on anything, all they had to do was ask and I was happy to do so.

Be excited! Nothing is worse than interviewing a person who speaks in a monotone voice and seems to be uncomfortable. You are interviewing to lead hundreds and potentially thousands of people. If you are openly nervous talking to five or ten people, how will you lead thousands? That's not to say you can control your nerves, but use that nervous energy to your advantage. Let the hiring team know how excited you are to be meeting with them and about the potential for working with them. You have one chance to make a first impression. If the first impression is that you come off as meek and insecure, that's how they will remember you. If you come into the room and light it up, they will remember that, too!

Most any leadership position you apply for is a people business, a relationship business. Your interview should focus on building professional relationships with staff and not about data. I have been involved in interviews where the candidate wants to talk about how, over the last three years, they improved the math scores at their school by three points. Nobody cares! When you are interviewing, people want to know how you are going to build a culture of success and a caring environment where people want to work. Focus your interview on building relationships, systems for communication, and your plan to build a team of professionals who will do everything possible to boost student success.

SECOND-ROUND INTERVIEWS

For most high-level jobs, the board or interview committee will have a second round of interviews. If you make it to the second round of an interview process, congratulations! That means you did your job in the first round and impressed interviewers enough that they want to meet with you again. But there may be one or two others who impressed them as well, so the second interview requires a different approach.

In almost every case, the second interview is a much less formal affair. Sometimes they want you to bring your spouse or family.

In most cases, they just want to meet your family and let them explore the district while they visit with you more. The most important part of this meeting is to not screw it up! A friend of mine took his wife to a second interview. At some point during the meeting, his wife asked a board member, who was a little over-weight, when her baby was due. The board member said, "Honey, I'm fifty-five years old. My baby is thirty-five." My friend's wife was understandably mortified, and my friend, incidentally, did not get the job.

In this second interview, the focus should be on interactions with the board. They want to know you are a good fit. They want to see how comfortable you are with them in an informal setting, and they want to see if whatever you did in the first interview to impress them is still there in the second interview. Remember, board members hire people they like. Do whatever you can to be honest and personable, and establish a comfortable rapport so they want to work with you.

CONTRACT NEGOTIATIONS

If you are selected as the finalist for a job, immediately turn to the contract and make sure all the formal and legal details of the new job are taken care of. You will probably already have had some discussions with the search consultant or the board president at this point about some details in the contract package, but now is the time to get it all in writing and formalized.

There are many things to consider in the contract, but the main elements are salary, length of the contract, and the variety of possible benefits—such as travel allowances, insurance, health savings accounts, 403(b)s, longevity pay, housing allowances, automatic raises, automatic contract renewals, and retirement reimbursement.

Depending on the district and where you are in your career, sometimes it is best to accept a lower salary and maximize benefits, due to tax implications. As you near retirement, most financial advisors will tell you to get everything possible into salary and take minimal benefits, because of long-term retirement implications. By balancing salary and benefits, you can come up with a package you and the board are happy with. I have only seen a time or two when the two sides could not agree on a fair contract.

Have a lawyer or an advisor on your team review the contract before it is finalized. A school attorney's job is to write a contract that is most beneficial to the district. They can write clauses and protections that give the board some freedoms to fire you, place you on leave, meet without you, and other terms you might find unacceptable. An attorney on your side can help make mutually beneficial contract adjustments.

LIVING IN THE DISTRICT

I will mention this briefly because it is important. If you are offered a job as the leader of a school district, make it a priority to live within the boundaries of the district. You will be setting the tax rate for the citizens and leading the schools, so I strongly believe you need to have "skin in the game" by living in the community.

There are certainly some exceptions—for example, the district is so rural that housing is not available, or property values are so high that a public school employee can't afford to live in the district. In those cases, it is not uncommon for the district to have a district-owned home for the superintendent, provide a housing allowance as part of the salary, or make it clear that they don't expect the superintendent to live in the district.

I have seen cases in which a school leader takes a new job but continues to live in another community, keeping their kids enrolled in a familiar school. I'm not saying it can't work, but it is not advisable. In large districts, this may not be as big a deal, but in smaller districts, it can be a source of contention. Do everything possible to let your board, staff, and community know you are committed to the job and not just passing through. Taking a job that pays you a six-figure salary should buy your new community some loyalty and trust, in my opinion. Establishing residence where you work and enrolling your kids in the school you lead offer a good start.

YOU GOT THE JOB—NOW WHAT?

After securing the job you worked so hard to get, you are in the driver's seat of a large organization, so everyone is watching to see how you plan to lead. You are now the dog that has finally caught the car it's been chasing, and you have to figure out what you are going to do with it! It is imperative to have a plan on the first day of the job for how you will begin the transition.

Whether you are new to the community or just the position, some basic steps are in order for getting off to a great start, prolonging your honeymoon period, and getting buy-in from your staff and community. I believe you should have plans for the first thirty days, first six months, and first year. These should be written and placed where you'll see them every day. By having them prominently in view, you can check off items one by one as you accomplish each part of the plan. I always gave my one-year plan to my board during my first-year evaluation as a reminder of what I told them I would accomplish. This provided visual proof that I actually did what I said I would do. By having a solid transition plan in writing, you will not forget or dismiss key steps along the way.

MEET WITH EVERYONE

It is important that you take the time to introduce yourself to everyone in your organization. Depending on when you are hired, this could be an end-of-year assembly, a convocation at the beginning of the year, or a video message that goes out to all staff—although I believe you should do these in person if possible. During my first meeting with all the staff, I properly introduced myself, talked about my family, and answered a lot of questions. Finally, I laid out some commonsense expectations I had for our school moving forward. Some of these came from my core beliefs, and others came from my interviews with staff, but I kept it simple and positive, doing what I could do to get buy-in from staff on day one.

Depending on the position, my next objective was to meet individually with every single person I would be in direct daily contact with. During the first week on the job, I had my secretary block off as many days as it took for me to set aside thirty minutes to meet with each person on my list. When I was a campus principal with a staff of about fifty, I met with each of them over the course of several days. When I became a superintendent, I met with each leader in the central office, each principal and director, and every key office staffer such as administrative assistants. If you are in a particularly large district, you may have to meet only with your cabinet and other direct reports. You know whom you should meet with, so have your assistant set up the meetings and get going!

During these individual meetings, I had a general introduction to let them tell me about themselves, and then we talked about the school, what they loved about it, and changes they would make if they were in charge. After meeting with all of these people, I easily found common themes that gave me a laundry list of what I call "low-hanging fruit."

LOW-HANGING FRUIT

Give some thought to what people's first impression of your leadership will be. From my prior discussions and overall view of a district when I arrived, I tried to find some low-hanging fruit—areas where I could make immediate changes that people would see.

Sometimes the low-hanging fruit involved mowing the grass and edging the sidewalks at campus entrances. You might be surprised at how something this simple can impact people. When parents drop their kids off at a freshly mown lawn with crisp edging, trimmed shrubs, and no trash, it makes a difference.

Adding coffee or frappuccino machines to staff lounges, adjusting schedules to allow colleagues to work together, making changes to duty stations and times, or a simple rolling cart with snacks for staff are all simple acts that establish healthy morale. In one district, I changed the summer work schedule from a five-day to a four-day week, and as you might imagine, this made lots of employees very happy.

POLICY REVIEW

Most school board organizations offer a policy review, which is very helpful. In this review, staff members go over every policy in your manual and scour it for mistakes as well as policies that are outdated or are no longer legal or necessary. When they come to your school, they will have a list of policies to go over with your administrative team and school board, working with you to clean them up.

This process will likely not have happened in many years because it is not a fun exercise. It is tedious, takes a lot of time, and requires your staff and board members to spend hours in a room together. However, when the process is done, district leadership and the school board will be on the same page as it pertains to school policy, and you will have likely cleaned up a lot of outdated policies in the process.

I recommend a full policy review during the first year or so of your tenure, but probably not in the first thirty days unless major policy issues need to be changed immediately.

FINANCIAL AUDIT

A financial audit is also sometimes necessary. Depending on the situation you are walking into, it may be necessary to hire an independent auditor to do a full financial audit of the school's finances. In many cases, the school's auditor has been working in the school district for many years. Nothing is necessarily wrong with that, but sometimes the auditor depends heavily on district staff to provide much of the data, without doing it themselves. This results in the auditor reporting only on what has been provided. That is not how this process is supposed to work.

One of my colleagues took over a school district as the assistant superintendent in charge of finance. Once she was on the job, things did not seem right to her. After ordering a third-party audit, she found that the district had been doing many things that were illegal, and she was in a real bind. She had to report to the superintendent and school board what she had found, which implicated the person she replaced, the school's longtime auditor, and put the district in crisis mode while they dug themselves out of a very serious financial bind.

Even though it is an extra cost and your current auditor will probably not be happy about it, it is never a bad idea to have a third party audit the district finances as you enter a new job. It verifies if the current auditor is doing a great job, or in some scenarios, it digs up significant problems you and your board need to know about. Either way, it sets a baseline for you in your new position.

LEADERSHIP MEETINGS

The next structure you should put in place is regular meetings with key administrative members. Again, depending on the size of your organization, there are many ways to structure this, and there is no right or wrong way. Deciding on who you meet with, the frequency of those meetings, and how those meetings operate will be very important. In my career, I basically used the following three administrative-type meetings— cabinet, administrative, and instructional. Let's discuss each, briefly.

Cabinet Meetings

The cabinet meeting is a meeting with your inner circle. For me, this was a relatively short meeting held every Monday morning to set the week, go over calendars, get feedback about any ongoing issues, and generally reinforce key actions that needed to happen that week. When I was at a very small school, my cabinet included my business manager, principal, and me. When I moved to a somewhat larger school, my cabinet consisted of my CFO, curriculum director, and me. And when I moved to the largest district in which I worked, my cabinet included my assistant superintendent of administrative services, assistant superintendent of business and operations, human resources director, communications director, and me. You will have to determine who is on your cabinet, but think of cabinet members as "direct reports" you count on to help you lead the district.

Administrative Meetings

I liked bringing in all my directors and principals for a monthly meeting to make sure we were all hearing the same information and could discuss important issues in a group setting. I included my directors of athletics, foodservice, transportation, custodial, technology, curriculum, finance, special education, and communications, as well as the principal of every campus. In my largest school, this was a meeting with about twenty-five staffers in attendance. Very large districts would likely omit principals from these meetings and find other ways to regularly communicate with them.

In these meetings, I had one rule. If you don't speak up during the meeting, you agree with what is being said. My philosophy was to always hire the smartest people I could, so I welcomed bright ideas. This was the culture I wanted to build around these meetings. I wanted my team to know I expected them to speak up if they did not agree, wanted to debate, or knew of a better way to do something. The final part of this rule was that if they didn't speak up, when we left the room, we were all in agreement. It takes some time to develop this level of trust with your team, but once you do, these meetings become a fun, inspirational means for making the absolute best decisions, with everyone feeling their opinions are heard and considered.

I started these meetings by going over whatever I wanted to cover for the month—key happenings, questions about projects, concerns, or something I had seen or heard. Then, I asked each director to give a quick synopsis of what was going on in their department and important things they needed to relay to the group. After they had given their report, the floor was open, so anyone in the room could ask questions—questions about why bus 22 is always late to school, why the cafeteria at ABC Elementary is running out of food, or why our custodial staff is not completing their work.

After the support directors had given their reports and answered questions, I allowed them to leave the meeting. I didn't want to waste their time by having them stuck in a room all day listening to issues and topics in which they had no interest or authority.

Instructional Meetings

Immediately after the administrative meeting, we took a short break, then those who were involved in instruction stayed for the second part of the meeting. This meeting included the assistant superintendent in charge of instruction, principals, curriculum director, special education director, technology director, and invited guests who were asked to present something to the group. This meeting was all about instruction and how we could do better at presenting our curriculum in the most efficient and effective ways for our students.

This was an important meeting for our principals because I wanted to make sure that, for instance, each elementary school provided the same high-quality education. It also allowed principals in elementary schools to see what was going on at the secondary level, and vice versa. The principals became close during this process, and it gave them a forum with district leadership to stress their need for support, personnel, or programs.

As mentioned, in really large districts, these meetings with principals might be best in a separate meeting.

DON'T WASTE TIME!

My general rule regarding meetings is to not waste people's time. Some districts have a weekly meeting with all the people mentioned in the meetings above. Taking a principal off their campus for one day each week is not a good use of their time. Don't make meetings longer or more frequent than they should be. If people go off on tangents or regurgitate fodder, move the meeting along. If one person seems to take over every meeting, pull them aside in private and let them know, in a nice way, that listening is just as important as talking.

Managing these meetings can be as important as the substance of the meetings. If members think of them as drudgery, the meetings will lose their effectiveness. Have an agenda, stick to it, manage the conversation and the pace of the meeting, and don't waste people's time. If you don't have anything to talk about or can put what you want to say in a brief email, do it. Leadership should look forward to attending and see these meetings as productive, informative, and helpful in moving the organization forward.

COMMUNITY OUTREACH

No matter the size of the community, as a school leader, you need to insert yourself into the community outside of school.

Church, civic organizations, youth leagues, and nonprofits are all groups looking for new members and that can earn you some goodwill in your community. Since the school is usually one of the largest employers in the area, as soon as you get settled in, you will likely be asked to become a board member of your local chamber of commerce, hospital, or other organizations.

Like so many things in this book, the size and type of community in which you work will help you decide how to best use your limited time. When I was at a small school district, I found the most popular and best-attended service organization in town and joined. This gave me a weekly lunch meeting with members of the community, and I enjoyed this one-hour respite from the office to help my community.

When I moved to a much larger community, I was on the chamber of commerce and local hospital boards, and I was the guest speaker at many different civic organizations. Since so many different organizations dotted this particular community, I didn't feel good about joining just one, so I went to them all at least once a year to interact with their members and give a "state of the district" talk.

I caution that everyone wants a piece of the school superintendent, and everyone wants you on their board, membership roll, or service organization. Do your research, ask the right questions, and choose how to best utilize your time. Learn to say "no" sometimes, or you will find yourself contributing your time to every board, organization, and committee in town.

NEWS, RADIO, AND TELEVISION

As soon as you arrive in a new community, reach out to local media. Most times, journalists will reach out to you first, upon finding out you will be moving to their community, so they usually make the initial contact. Take advantage of their enthusiasm, and sit down personally with the local editor, education writer, radio personality, and television reporter, if possible.

If you can establish a good relationship and they genuinely like you, believe you are honest with them, and have access to you even in tough times, most media professionals will treat you fairly. That doesn't mean they won't report on touchy subjects or print negative information, but they will at least call for quotes so you can share your position on any given matter.

The vast majority of media professionals are good, decent people trying to do their jobs to the best of their ability. If you can build a certain level of mutual respect, there is a good chance the local media will be an ally and not an adversary.

STRATEGIC PLANNING

In the first year or so in your new position, go through a strategic planning process. Unless your new school has done an extraordinary job, you will likely find there is no plan, or if there is, it is on a shelf somewhere and no one really knows what is in it. In my opinion, the strategic plan should be the blueprint for your district's future. It should be used to make decisions, build a budget, and prompt topics of conversation at virtually every admin and board meeting.

If you ask community members what the future holds for their school district, most will tell you they have no idea. My goal through strategic planning was to produce a roadmap to the future. This roadmap had specific goals and tasks, and we had regular updates on our website and in public meetings, chronicling each time we completed a task. If someone wanted to know where the district was headed, it was right there in front of them.

For a successful strategic plan, you have to set it up correctly, involving a large group of people who represent your staff, community, parents, and students. You are recruiting brand ambassadors who will go out and promote your school's goals and achievements. Having a hundred people on the streets every day talking about the wonderful things going on in your school is much more valuable than any ad campaign.

It is also helpful to have a third party serve as the leader for this strategic plan. It can certainly be done in-house, but if the superintendent is leading the planning, many people might believe they are just focusing on topics they are interested in and that it is not really an open process. Having someone who is not from your district to lead the meetings promotes open dialogue and buy-in within the group.

The key to any strategic plan is to make it a working document that is reviewed consistently. Once you have a plan in place, it should be on the board agenda several times a year for updates, constantly available to the public on the school's website, and discussed at admin and staff meetings throughout the district.

The goals of your district regarding academics, technology, facilities, and many other facets of education should be readily available for anyone interested in knowing the direction your district is moving.

FOLLOW UP AND MONITOR THE PLAN

Perhaps the most important part of the transition plan described above is to constantly follow up, keep it in front of you, and monitor it closely. You can choose how this works best for you, but I always liked to leave a one-page summary of my transition plans somewhere on my desk where I could see them every day. If you have a glass top on your desk, slide a copy of it under the glass so it is in your peripheral vision as you work. Leave it in your daily mailbox, or have it on your computer or phone as a tagged item. However you choose to make your goals part of your daily use is your choice. Just make sure you do it!

CONCLUSION

I HOPE THIS BOOK HAS PROVIDED CONCRETE PLANS AND examples of how using good commonsense techniques for leadership can work, even in a chaotic world. Further, I have shared some ways to get your foot in the door for a new job, interview techniques, and ways to make yourself stand out in a crowded field of quality applicants. Finally, I have given you a blueprint for what to do once you land that job and commonsense approaches to making a good transition, creating buy-in from your staff and community, and getting off to a great start in your new position.

Leadership does not have to be a complicated mess of philosophies, theories, store-bought programs, matrices, and rubrics. I believe that going back to the basics of building relationships, setting high expectations for students and staff, and having effective ways to communicate and monitor improvement and morale are all that is needed to build and maintain a wonderful work environment and a highly successful organization.

I hope you will use this book as a reference, as a book study, for groupthink sessions, as aspiring leader material, and in other productive ways to spread the message that despite how complicated our world gets, common sense can be used to lead great organizations. Public schools might continue to be pressured by fringe groups, politicians, and others wanting to disrupt the public education system for personal gain and to help their cronies. Behind the scenes, these groups are only after money. By using the tools and simple ideas presented in this book, you are well on your way to becoming a positive commonsense leader for your team. In fact, commonsense leaders, politicians, and citizens may be the only way out of this current state of chaos.

CHAPTER INDEX

www.ingramcontent.com/pod-product-compliance
Lightning Source LLC
Chambersburg PA
CBHW031850200326
41597CB00012B/342